CHANGES IN FAMILY LIFE

SIR WILLIAM BEVERIDGE
AND OTHERS

LONDON AND NEW YORK

First published in 1932

This edition first published in 2015
by Routledge
2 Park Square, Milton Park, Abingdon, Oxon, OX14 4RN

and by Routledge
711 Third Avenue, New York, NY 10017

Routledge is an imprint of the Taylor & Francis Group, an informa business

© 1932 William H. Beveridge

All rights reserved. No part of this book may be reprinted or reproduced or utilised in any form or by any electronic, mechanical, or other means, now known or hereafter invented, including photocopying and recording, or in any information storage or retrieval system, without permission in writing from the publishers.

Trademark notice: Product or corporate names may be trademarks or registered trademarks, and are used only for identification and explanation without intent to infringe.

British Library Cataloguing in Publication Data
A catalogue record for this book is available from the British Library

ISBN: 978-1-138-82643-4 (Set)
eISBN: 978-1-315-73730-0 (Set)
ISBN: 978-1-138-82822-3 (Volume 1)
eISBN: 978-1-315-73848-2 (Volume 1)
Pb ISBN: 978-1-138-82870-4 (Volume 1)

Publisher's Note
The publisher has gone to great lengths to ensure the quality of this reprint but points out that some imperfections in the original copies may be apparent.

Disclaimer
The publisher has made every effort to trace copyright holders and would welcome correspondence from those they have been unable to trace.

CHANGES IN FAMILY LIFE

by

SIR WILLIAM BEVERIDGE
AND OTHERS

LONDON
GEORGE ALLEN & UNWIN LTD
MUSEUM STREET

FIRST PUBLISHED IN 1932

All rights reserved
PRINTED IN GREAT BRITAIN BY
UNWIN BROTHERS LTD., WOKING

PREFACE

THE seven wireless talks printed in this volume were given between February 17th and April 7th, 1932. Four of the talks were monologues by myself; three were dialogues, involving, in addition to myself, Mrs. J. L. Adamson (a member of the National Executive of the Labour Party), Mrs. Eleanor Barton (General Secretary of the Women's Co-operative Guild), Dr. Hugh Dalton (Reader in Economics in the University of London), and Professor Morris Ginsberg (Martin White Professor of Sociology in the University of London).

In printing the talks one change of order has been made, bringing first three monologues, then three dialogues, and last another monologue summing up my first impressions of the returns received. Those are first impressions only; analysis of the returns will be matter for another volume, which cannot be published for many months. Each of the first three monologues, as spoken, contained passages explaining the scheme of investigation, defending it against criticism, or inviting listeners to send for the Family Form and fill it up. In printing the talks these passages have been omitted as no longer needed; so far as they appear at all in this volume they appear below in this Preface. On the other hand, the talks have in other directions been amplified by inclusion of statistical passages or references to the charts printed here, but incommunicable through the microphone. The three dialogues are printed practically as they were spoken, with slight revision and amplification in the first of them.

The dialogues are to be taken as conversation. In these particular dialogues, as in ordinary conversation, the interlocutors have at times, for the sake of the argument, put points of view that seemed to them reasonable at the time as worth exploring, rather than final and considered judgments to which they individually would at all times subscribe. The degree to which microphone dialogues should differ from ordinary conversation in this respect is one of the many problems raised by this new medium.

The talks were arranged as part of a scheme of social investigation, whose genesis was briefly as follows. Last July I was approached by representatives of the adult education side of the British Broadcasting Corporation, who said that they were anxious to carry further and into a new field attempts already made by them to secure the interest and help of listeners in collecting information of scientific interest. These attempts, which hitherto had been made on a small scale, and related to comparatively simple facts of natural science, had received an encouraging response. The B.B.C. now contemplated, as an appendage to a general programme of educational talks on "The Changing World," an investigation in social science—specifically, a study of recent changes in family life. If the B.B.C. arranged

PREFACE

the talks, and undertook the distribution and collection of a form of questions, would I, besides taking some part in the talks, undertake without cost to the B.B.C. the analysis of the returns received? My answer was that if the form of questions were such as to hold out hope of getting facts of value for social science, I thought that the analysis could be undertaken by drawing on research funds available in the School of Economics; if very few answers were received, the cost of analysing them would be small; if many were received, their value for scientific purposes would be more than proportionately increased. It was agreed, also, in order to issue the form without charge to those who asked for it and thus improve the chance of a large response, that the cost of printing should be provided from the funds of the School; the B.B.C. had covered the cost of previous questionnaires by a small charge to those who sent for them. The plan of talks and investigation was provisionally approved and was announced in the B.B.C.'s programme of winter talks called *The Changing World*, published in September 1931.

The actual talks to be given and form of questions to be issued were not settled till much later. The form, after some preliminary discussion by an informal Committee summoned by the B.B.C., was ultimately drafted in November, by myself, though with abundant help from other members of the School of Economics. It was discussed and, after various amendments, was approved by the Central Council for Broadcast Adult Education and conditions of issue were laid down, to preserve the voluntary character of the investigation and the anonymity of the returns received. The Family Form was not to be obtruded on anyone, just because he was a listener or a reader of the weekly papers issued by the B.B.C. It was to be sent only to individuals who wrote to ask for it or to societies co-operating with the B.B.C., which themselves undertook the responsibility of bringing the form to the notice of their members. The returned forms were to be sent to the B.B.C. in special envelopes on which the sender was invited to put his name (or initials) and address for communications. The B.B.C. would put an identical number on envelope and form and then separate them, retaining the envelope, and sending on the anonymous form to the School of Economics for examination. This plan, it may be said in passing, has worked admirably.

The use of the co-operating societies for distribution of the forms has also worked well, but had one unexpected by-product.

In order to give these societies time to get the Family Form into the hands of their members before the talks began on February 17th, supplies of the form had to be sent to them three weeks in advance. As this would in fact have made the form public property, it was thought advisable at the same time officially to issue it to the Press with a brief covering note. It was received by the greater part of the Press with extreme disfavour; in Fleet Street, the form produced something like an explosion, extending even to the usually calmer regions of Printing House Square. Nearly all the London papers were either critical or contemptuous of the scheme; the provincial Press, as it is called, was more divided and gave in some cases strong and reasoned support, while the London papers gave publicity by opposition. The only extensive publicity originally contemplated for the scheme of investigation was that to be obtained through the microphone, with full accompanying explanations. The interest of the Press came to me at least as a complete surprise. The net result was to cause more than 15,000 copies of the Family Form to be issued before the first talk had been given. The total issue, of 50,000, by the end of March had altogether exceeded any of the original estimates of requirements, which ranged round 10,000 or 20,000.

The number of forms completed and returned at the time of writing is of course only a small proportion of the issue, and was never expected to be a large proportion. Listeners were advised through the microphone to send for the form as an accompaniment of the talks, even though they did not contemplate making a return. The form itself, as may be judged from the Appendix by any who have not seen it, was a long and apparently complicated affair. It is possible that general Press support would have caused a larger proportion of the forms issued to be returned. On the other hand, it is probable that general support would not have given equal publicity to the talks or caused quite so many forms to be issued. On balance, the Press attitude has probably made little difference to the working of the scheme.

It would be idle, however, at this date to pursue this question and worse than idle to revive a dying controversy by replying to any of the criticisms made last February. As I said in the talk on Nature and Nurture, the scheme is a sober attempt by the help of listeners and the power of the microphone "to construct a new kind of instrument for social science." In social science we can hardly make deliberate experiments at all. We must get our facts by observation and must depend on number of observations to eliminate factors irrelevant to any particular enquiry. We can, of course, by a compulsory inquisition like the census get observations in large numbers. But the questions that we can put into a compulsory census are rigidly limited by public opinion. They must, moreover, be questions which every citizen can fairly be compelled to answer truthfully under penalties. Over a large range of social studies we must depend on answers given voluntarily: if we are to get such answers in large numbers we are driven to the use of forms and to trying to persuade ordinary citizens to fill them up for us. The alternative to succeeding in such a venture may be blank ignorance.

How far the particular venture illustrated in this volume has succeeded it is too soon to say. Some success at least can be claimed for it. The 8,000 family returns already received, covering 20,000 families and 200,000 persons, represent a large mass of facts of absorbing interest; they are a record of family life, among all sorts and conditions of men, in this generation and the last, which it may take years of study to exhaust completely. Whether the number of returns, when split up by date or economic grade, will be sufficient to furnish scientific conclusions on questions of human biology is another matter. It would be absurd even to hazard an opinion on that, either favourable or unfavourable, till the material has been examined.

Nor is the enquiry itself in any sense complete. Copies of the Family Form may still be obtained free of charge from the Publications Department of the B.B.C., and if they are returned at any time within the next six months, they can be used in our calculations. There is still time to add to the power of our instrument. More than that, the Family Form itself is only one stage of enquiry. A large proportion, nearly a quarter of those who have returned the form, have expressed their desire to assist in the further investigations forecast in it. It may be that we have laid the foundations of a continuing study of changing social conditions such as has never before been possible.

Whether this has been done or not, whatever

comes of the scheme of investigation, I hope that the talks will have served the purpose of helping men and women throughout the country to think over the problems that centre round the fundamental institution of the Family, and to be prepared to deal with those problems, individually or collectively, as occasion calls with broader views and more balanced judgment.

W. H. B.

April 1932

CONTENTS

CHAPTER	PAGE
PREFACE	7
I. THE CHANGING FAMILY	19
II. THE FAMILY AND THE POPULATION QUESTION	32
III. NATURE AND NURTURE	51
IV. THE ECONOMICS OF FAMILY LIFE	67
V. THE FAMILY AS A SOCIAL GROUP	83
VI. SOME PROBLEMS FOR SOLUTION	103
VII. THE ENDURING FAMILY: A FIRST IMPRESSION OF THE RETURNS	121
APPENDIX: THE FAMILY FORM	141
INDEX	157

CHARTS

	PAGE
I. AGE OF MARRIAGE IN ENGLAND AND WALES, 1896 TO 1930	35
II. BIRTHS, MARRIAGES, AND REAL INCOME	45
III. MARRIED WOMEN'S EMPLOYMENT IN 1911 AND 1921	76
IV. CONSENT OF BRIDE TO MARRIAGE IN VARIOUS SOCIAL STAGES	88
V. ADMISSIONS TO LINCOLN'S INN, 1886 TO 1927 (*The above are re-produced by courtesy of "The Listener."*)	97
VI. PROPORTIONATE DISTRIBUTION OF POPULATION, WIRELESS LICENCES AND FAMILY RETURNS	124

CHANGES IN FAMILY LIFE

I

THE CHANGING FAMILY

Suppose that each one of us were asked to make a list of the outstanding events or governing influences in his or her life. What would that list contain? Each of us, according to our age and our life's experiences, might speak of different things. But for nearly all of us most of these things would arise out of the relationships into which we were born, or which had been made for us later by marriage. They would be family influences and events: the guidance or example of father or mother, the accidents or decisions leading to marriage, marriage itself, a birth, a death, an unhoped-for recovery from illness of one nearly lost to us, a separation or a coming together, the interest of watching and planning for the new generation. Some of us would name also an event connected with our occupations in peace or in war, would recall the influence of a teacher, or would dwell on the memory of a comradeship in work. Some might find a place for the reading of a book, or the hearing of a speech, or sermon. For a few people life gets filled by an absorbing vocation, or a vital friendship outside the family;

for all the rest, something connected with family would come high in the list; for a great majority, it would come first; for many, it might make up the whole list.

That is true, I believe, about men no less than about women. It is true of men and women, irrespective of their occupation or their station in life; it is true about men and women, not of one race, or country, or colour, but of all. What matters vitally to nearly every human being is the handful of other human beings to whom he is linked by birth or marriage, not the indifferent millions with whom he shares this changing world.

What matters to the individual is other individuals, rather than the general mould of law and custom in which his relations to them are cast. Whatever the formal relation of husband and wife, parent and child, brother and sister, whatever their legal rights over one another, and over the family income by which they live, their actual relations and rights are always a matter of private arrangement. The Roman father has come down to us through history as the type of all that is absolute and tyrannical in the power of one human being over others, over his wife and children as over his slaves. But we may be sure that often the Roman father, when he had done something of which the Roman mother was not likely to approve, went in terror before her, and that often, too, the Roman father spent hours upon his knees before the Roman baby, appeasing its anger and cajoling it to be good. We may be just as sure that Roman wives and mothers in the mass did not resent their legal subjection with the bitterness which their successors might feel to-day. They took it as part of the natural order, and would have resisted any change.

This does not mean that the laws and customs regulating family life do not matter. Far from it. Though each individual family is a private arrangement, the kind of arrangement that most individuals make depends upon public opinion; the law, in turn, influences public opinion, and expresses it. Again, when anything goes wrong in the private arrangement between individuals in a family, the law or custom determining their respective rights becomes important. The differences in the law or custom of the Family from one country to another, and its changes from one time to another, are important in themselves and are fascinating to study.

Mating and birth are the same for all men at all times. By these unchanging processes the human race is carried on. But the institutions which centre round these unchanging processes, themselves change continually. A recent writer on this subject has presented these changes as a development through three stages.[1]

The first stage is the kinship or tribal stage.

[1] Dr. Müller-Lyer in *The Family* (first published, in German, in 1912; English translation by F. W. Stella Browne, 1931).

Among many primitive peoples the tribe or clan counts more than the single family. The tribe is based on blood-relationship, but our sharp modern distinction between having common parents and having remoter ties of kinship does not hold; to be cousins means for many purposes as much as to be sibs (that is, to be brother or sister). Relationship is often counted through the mother rather than through the father. The woman who marries does not necessarily leave her group, nor does her husband leave his group.

The second stage is the full family stage. Here, under the dominance of one male, the family forms a closely knit group for all purposes, social, political, and economic. In republican Rome the father was the absolute owner of his wife and children and slaves alike, of all they made and all they earned; they had no relations with the world outside. The family was the indivisible atom of which society was made. For another people this stage is summed up by the statements that an Englishman's house is his castle, and that every woman's place is in a castle of this kind. Most races that have progressed and made civilization have also at one time or other taken this strong patriarchal view, have based the family on the undisputed dominance of the father.

The third stage is described by this writer as the personal stage, not yet wholly achieved anywhere, but gradually coming upon us. The development of manufacturing and trade deprives the household of many of its former functions. The State undertakes duties that were formerly those of the family, such as education, or provision for old age. The personalities of wife and children claim and get independent recognition from the State. The family becomes less closely knit, less dominated by one member, perhaps less permanent. The atom seems to be breaking up a little.

These are the three stages in general terms. Let me illustrate them by three particular communities— by the Trobriand Islanders of to-day for the kinship stage, by ourselves last century for the full family stage, by ourselves to-day for the personal stage, not yet come but casting its shadow before.

The Trobrianders, whom I take as typical for the kinship stage of family life, are people now living in two small islands off the coast of New Guinea. They have just been the subject of study by Dr. Malinowski, Professor of Anthropology in the University of London.[1]

The Trobrianders are savages; they do many things that we should regard as immoral. They have no law against polygamy, and the chiefs do, in fact, each have a number of wives. But the chiefs are exceptional. The normal family among the Trobrianders is a family of one husband and one wife united in enduring companionship, and in

[1] The account given here of the Trobrianders is based entirely on Dr. Malinowski's book on *The Sexual Life of Savages* (1932).

the care of children. Dr. Malinowski has brought back photographs of Trobriand family groups in essentials like those which nearly all of us possess in our family albums, of family visits to the seaside in the summer. And he has recorded expressions of love between two persons, and of domestic life and affection among these savages exactly as we understand it.

But with this similarity in fundamental relations there go some very odd differences. The Trobriand community, in the language of anthropologists, is patrilocal and matrilineal. Patrilocal means that the family lives in the father's village; the wife moves from her own village to her husband's on marriage, and there the children are born and reared. The Trobrianders are patrilocal as we are. Matrilineal means that the Trobrianders count descent through the mother, not as we do, or have done, through the father; they carry this to the point of denying any relationship between a father and his children at all. The most sacred duty of a Trobriand man is to provide not for his own children, but throughout her life for his sister and her children. When a woman marries and goes to live with her husband, her brothers send after her, year by year, a supply of food. They are the nearest male relations and guardians of her children. Her husband is not their guardian, or any relation. We have all heard of the little girl in England who, when asked who her father was, replied, "He is the gentleman that lives with mother." That is what he is in literal fact to the Trobriand child. A chief who dies cannot be succeeded by his son. His heir is either his brother (born of the same mother) or a nephew (born of his sister). When the children grow up in their father's village, they find themselves strangers, living there on sufferance. Dr. Malinowski gives a striking account of a quarrel between a son of one of the chiefs and a nephew, leading to the expulsion of the son from his father's village. The chief was very fond of his son, as Trobriand fathers generally are, in spite of thinking that their sons are no relations. But in this quarrel the chief could do nothing whatever to save his son from expulsion. He could only sulk at his nephew and the rest of his real relations.

Some people may think that these Trobrianders, however interesting in themselves, have little to do with Britain. To my mind, however, that story of the quarrel is full of morals for us. In normal family life the Trobriand savages are more like us than they are in anything else, because normal family life rests on universal human needs. But when anything goes wrong in the family and a quarrel comes, the result may be quite different, in different communities, because the law is different. That is one of the main points of this opening chapter. Again, to deny relationship between a father and his children, as the Trobrianders do, sounds to us fantastic. But we British need not go far afield to find something that to-day seems almost equally fantastic, though in another way from that of the Trobrianders. We have only to look at my second community, in the full family stage, also islanders. They are the islanders who lived in the south of Britain during the first half of the nineteenth century.

The Trobriand father to-day has no rights over his children. Less than a hundred years ago a married mother in England had no rights over hers. It needed an Act of Parliament in 1839 to give a married woman whose children had been taken away from her by her husband for no reason, the right of getting an order of the Court which would allow her to visit them occasionally. It needed another Act of Parliament, nearly fifty years later, to give the mother any rights of guardianship at all. Till 1886 her husband, who had the sole guardianship of the children during his life, could by will appoint someone other than the mother as guardian after his death. The mother did not get equal rights with the father in guardianship and appointment of guardians till 1926—till six years ago.

The law of succession was almost as one-sided against the mother as the law of guardianship. To-day, if a person dies without a will, father and mother stand on equal terms to inherit from him; but that equality in our law is just seven years old.

Of course, these laws of the English islanders did not rest on the view that the mother had nothing to do with bringing her children into the world.

What they rested on was the doctrine that no woman could properly have children except by ceasing to be legally a person. By marriage she became for all purposes, legal, political, and economic, part of her husband, like one of his ribs restored to him. If someone gave a piece of land to Mr. Smith and Mrs. Smith and Miss Jones, whom we should now regard as three persons, the law divided the land not into three parts but into two: Miss Jones as one person got one half; Mr. and Mrs. Smith, as also one person, got the other half. Mr. and Mrs. Smith's half, of course, went wholly to Mr. Smith. In the law's curious arithmetic, Miss Jones = 1 because she is single; Mr. Smith = 1 because he is a man; Mrs. Smith = 0. On marriage a woman's personal property of every kind passed to her husband, and she could never during his life hold any such property again; every investment that she held, and every penny that she earned, became his automatically, could be spent by him, could be willed away from her at his death; her real property—that is, land and houses—did not become his so completely, but was completely under his control. It was only fifty years ago that the property of married women generally was assured to them. It was forty-one years ago that by judicial decision a husband's power to imprison his wife at home was formally taken from him.[1] That was the last relic of the

---

[1] Decision of the Court of Appeal in *The Queen* versus *Jackson* ([1891] 1 Q.B. 671). In this case, which became known as

husband's lordship over his wife, which till 1790 made it treason punished by burning alive for a wife to kill her husband; for a husband to kill his wife was never more than simple murder.

The change of family law in the past century is remarkable. The change affects far more than the personal relations of husband and wife. It touches the position of children, where the parents' control was formerly unrestricted. It touches the permanence of marriage, since divorce was first made possible in 1857. As regards liberty of the wife, the change

"The Clitheroe Case," Mr. Jackson with the help of some friends seized Mrs. Jackson, who had left him, as she was leaving church on Sunday, carried her off in a carriage and left her, confined under the care of a nurse, till she should agree to live with him. The Court of Appeal granted a writ of *habeas corpus* compelling him to release her. In so doing they overruled a judgment given in 1840 in *The Matter of Cochrane*, in which it had been held that "where a wife absents herself from her husband, on account of no misconduct on his part, and he afterwards, by a stratagem, obtains possession of her person, and she declares her intention of leaving him again whenever she can, he has a right to restrain her of her liberty, until she is willing to return to a performance of her conjugal duties." "Mrs. Cochrane," said Mr. Justice Coleridge in that case, "has lived apart from her husband for nearly four years, without loss of character, but she must allow me to say that her husband, with the highest opinion of her virtue, might yet be excused, even by her, if he felt uneasy when he learned . . . that she had gone to masked balls in Paris with persons whom he did not know. He may well be desirous, and he has a right, to restrain her from the power to frequent such amusements, unprotected by his presence and without his permission . . . Let her be restored to Mr. Cochrane." Cochrane's case presumably remained good law till 1891.

has recently been summed up by a judge in a case which most people will remember:—

"No man to-day can make himself the owner of a woman under the guise of a marriage service. A married woman in this country has gained her freedom. She is a citizen, and not a servant. She can exercise her own judgment. She can choose her part. She can decide her own future."[1]

That is an interesting and provocative statement of the law. It has made us all wonder where the family is going.

But we must not exaggerate the effect of changes in the law alone. To look only at the legal structure of the family and its changes is to miss most of the truth, and that for two reasons.

The first reason has already been suggested. To most families for most of the time the law does not matter; the relations of its members rest on private arrangement. The law makes a difference only when things go badly, when the private arrangement of the family breaks up and the members appeal to outside authority. Millions of Victorian wives knew that if the law counted them equal to naught, their husbands thought otherwise; that if the law called them servants, the law was an ass—they were partners. Some wives of to-day feel that, though the law may call them free and equal, they are still in the chains of economic dependence.

This brings me to the second reason for looking

[1] Mr. Justice McCardie in *Place* v. *Searle*, as reported in the *Daily Telegraph*, January 20th, 1932.

beyond the law in studying changes of family life. Among the general forces that can affect the family, legal changes are only one, and not the most important. While in the past fifty years the law of the family has been transformed, there have been other changes which in practice have made more difference. There has been, first, a change, amounting to a vital revolution, in the normal size of the family. How this affects on the one hand the population question generally, and on the other hand the life of individual family groups, will be one of the topics of the next chapter. There has been, second, a transformation of economic conditions in Britain, a change in the openings for work outside the home, and a change of work requiring to be done in the home.

The Married Women's Property Act of 1882 has often been described as a revolution, but chiefly by those who thought only of the richer classes, only of the few people with enough property to make a difference in their lives. For the great bulk of married women in this country that is not the case; for them the important question is not whether any possessions they may have, or any money they earn, are legally theirs, or not, but how the family income comes, and how it is distributed. If a dispute arises, the degree of their dependence upon their husband's will, or the power to take an independent line, depends not on the possession of property, or the reverse, but on whether there are for them any opportunities for earning outside the home.

Victorian husbands and wives and children were in many respects more like those of to-day than the change of their legal position suggests; in other respects, untouched by law, their lives were very different. If we are to get a true picture of social development, we must study, not legal structure alone, but all sides of the Family.

How can that be done? It cannot be done from the law books, and it cannot be done by looking at the census, or at returns of births, deaths, and marriages; in later chapters I shall try to show both what may be learned of interest from these official records and where they fail. It cannot be done by any kind of official compulsory enquiry. It can be done if a large number of individuals will voluntarily, under due safeguards, give information which they alone can give. That is the purpose of the B.B.C. investigation by means of the Family Form.[1]

[1] Printed as an Appendix, p. 141–155.

II

THE FAMILY AND THE POPULATION QUESTION

AFTER the preliminary or Reference Section A in the Family Form, the first question asked, in Section B, is the date of the marriage. What we are trying to discover is the changes that have come over family life in the last fifty years. We must have all our facts dated.

The next two questions are the dates of birth of husband and wife, so as to get their ages at marriage. Those are two facts of fundamental importance.

Upon the ages of the partners at marriage depends the kind of partnership on which they set out—whether the partnership is likely to be long or short, whether it is to be one of discovering the world together, or one of welding two careers that are already settling into shape, what kind of companion each can easily be to the other, what are their prospects of having children, how much older they are going to be than their children, and how that will affect their relations and mutual understanding.

Everybody has a theory as to the ideal age for marriage, and of how the ages of the partners should compare. Everybody has a theory, from the Greek philosopher Aristotle downwards. "Women," said Aristotle, "should marry when they are about eighteen years of age, and men at seven-and-thirty, for then they are in the prime of life, and the decay of the powers of both will coincide." I do not suppose, for a moment, that Aristotle carried out his theory in his own case; marriage is a matter in which people seldom carry out their theories. Let us drop theories and come to facts: when do people marry to-day?

We know something about that from the Reports of the Registrar-General. Let us take only marriages of bachelors and spinsters—about 90 per cent. of the whole in each case. Widows and widowers naturally marry later. That is why it is important to know, and why we ask in the form, whether the marriage is a first marriage or not; the details of any earlier marriage can be given in section C, but the details are not so important.

Let me come back to the Registrar-General. The average age for bachelors to marry in England and Wales is now twenty-seven years and four months. The average age for spinsters is twenty-five years and six months. A generation ago, in 1896, both sexes married earlier in life; bachelors about nine months earlier and spinsters about five months earlier. But though this is the result if we compare 1930 with 1896, if we look at the time between those years we find an interesting contrast. Up to the war the age of marriage was rising steadily for both sexes; in the war and just after, it went up and down erratically; but from 1922 onwards it has been definitely lower than it was just before the war; it has also been falling steadily for men and falling also, though less markedly, for women. To-day, both men and women are marrying earlier than they did just before the war. The former tendency to postponement of marriage seems to have been reversed.

These figures are set out graphically in Chart I, showing the average ages of marriage of bachelors and of spinsters, in England and Wales, for each year from 1896 to 1930. The figures themselves can be found in the annual Reports of the Registrar-General. The rise for both sexes till just before the war is remarkably steady. It is interesting also to note that for both sexes the rise appears to be checked before the first of the war years; the age in 1913 is no higher than in 1912 for bachelors, while for spinsters it is lower; that is the first drop for many years. It is possible, therefore, that the lower age of marriage after the war is not a consequence of the war, but would have come in any case. That is one of the points for further enquiry, in this very interesting movement of the age of marriage.

Further enquiry is needed, for the general averages from the Registrar-General's Reports do not take us far.[1] They lump all the different occupations

[1] In addition to the difficulty mentioned in the text of the occupations being lumped together, there is the problem of the changing age constitution of the population. The pro-

THE FAMILY AND POPULATION QUESTION 35

CHART I

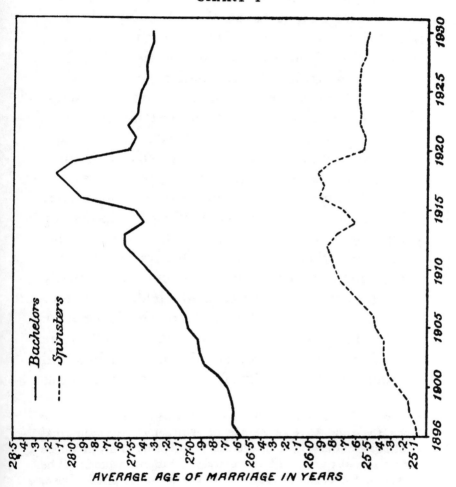

together—agricultural, industrial, trading, professional. We know, from the census and in other ways, that the normal age of marriage differs from one kind of occupation to another. Broadly, the less skilled workmen tend to marry earlier than the more skilled. That is a natural reflection of the fact that, the less skilled the occupation, the earlier do those following it begin to earn the full adult wage and feel themselves able to support families. The same consideration makes the age of marriage earlier among manual workers than among the professional classes, whose full earning power may not begin till many years after they have reached manhood.

There are other reasons tending to hasten or postpone marriage in particular occupations. And since there are those differences between occupations, we can learn little of what is really happening from an average in which all occupations are lumped together. Here, as elsewhere, we have got to break up the general average. How has the age of marriage moved, not for all bachelors and spinsters in the lump, but for particular occupations

portions of marriageable men at various ages, in the decade since the war, have of course been upset by the abnormal death-rate of the war itself, and this would presumably influence indirectly also the age of marriage among women. The Registrar-General, in addition to the averages cited above, gives a useful and interesting table showing the marriage-rate at various age-groups. From these it looks as if there was a real tendency for marriage to come earlier in life. But this cannot yet be taken as established.

or districts? Are the former differences between occupations becoming less or greater? How is the age of marriage affected by differences in the chances of employment for women, before marriage and after? That is the sort of point on which our enquiry may throw light.

That economic conditions affect marriage in many ways is well known. It is easier (or in the past it has been easier) for people to marry when trade was good and there was plenty of employment; ever since the middle of the nineteenth century the marriage-rate—that is to say, the number of marriages per thousand of the population—has risen and fallen with the booms and depressions of the trade cycle; before that, when England was still largely an agricultural country, it was said that marriages rose and fell according as the harvest was good or bad.

The harvest certainly determined the time of year usually chosen for marriage. In most agricultural counties of England, marriages are most frequent in the last quarter of the year, when the work of the grain harvest is over, and the extra money earned then has been received. A few agricultural counties, chiefly pastoral, are an exception to this, and have most marriages, not in the last quarter of the year, but in the second quarter. So do, or did, a number of mining districts, where work slackens in spring, after the time of best earning in winter; since the war, there may have been a change in this. In most industrial districts seasonal fluctuation of employment goes the other way than with mining; harvests do not matter, and most marriages occur neither in the last quarter, nor in the second, but in the third quarter, the holiday season; Lancashire, Cheshire, and London, with its neighbouring counties, are all like that. As England in the last hundred years has become industrialized, proportionately more and more people have come to live in towns in place of living in the country. If therefore one lumps all the districts and all the population of England together, there comes a point at which the marriage season seems to change; up to 1890 the last quarter appears busiest, but from then onwards the third quarter. When those figures were first brought to my notice by a research student at the School of Economics,[1] I wondered what had brought about this change of our marrying habits. Why in 1890 had brides taken to name the day differently? But really, so far as one can judge, there is no change of habits at all; the people dependent on harvests have gone on marrying for choice just after the harvest, as they had probably done for centuries, while they were almost the whole population of England; the townspeople have also gone on as before, affected by holidays rather than by harvests, but at a certain

[1] The facts cited here are taken from an article on "Marriage Seasons," by Miss Dorothy S. Thomas, in *Economica*, February 1924. They relate to the period before the war; it would be interesting to bring them up to date.

THE FAMILY AND POPULATION QUESTION

point the townpeople came to be so numerous that they outweighed the country in the figures for England as a whole. That is another illustration, and a very good illustration, of what I said before about the danger of trusting to general averages.

The swing-over of England from rural to industrial pursuits has not only changed the apparent marriage season. It had also a more important result, in its influence on the number of the population. As is well known, the nineteenth century witnessed a rapid growth in the population of Britain. One of the explanations commonly given for this is that the growth of industry made earlier marriage possible. In a stable rural community house-room is limited; young couples may have to wait till a cottage becomes available before they can marry and establish a home and family. The Industrial Revolution broke up these restrictions on early marriage; the new factories wanted labourers and new houses would be built to accommodate them; young people no longer had to wait to step into the cottage of an older pair. They married sooner, and through that, among other reasons, an increase of population followed.

I am not sure that that view can be taken as established. What happened to population a hundred and fifty years ago must be to some extent matter for conjecture. We have not the facts and we cannot now get them. But we ought to be able to get all the facts needed to-day about population problems.

That brings me to the most important section of the form—the essence of the family—the children. In section D people are asked to enter all the children born of the marriage recorded in section B and to give some simple facts about them—date of birth, date of death if no longer living, whether they are still living at home, and, if not, when they left home, the kind of education they got, any scholarships they won.

At first sight this bit of the form looks like a census return. What can it tell us that last year's census did not tell us?

If one looks at it again, one sees that, even apart from the questions about scholarships and education, the form is not like the official census. It tells us about something quite different. The official census is concerned with households—it is a record of all the people sleeping under one roof on one particular night. Any child that has left home or is away at school or on a visit is not included with its family but somewhere else; any visitor or domestic servant is included. So too children no longer living do not appear in the official census. That is a census of households at one moment of time. The family form is concerned with something different— families and their history. It will tell us, if we can get it filled up by enough people, any number of important things that the official census cannot tell us.

Some of these things are related to the topics of later chapters rather than of this one. Questions as to education or the age of leaving home, for instance, concern the social side of the family rather than its vital side. These questions appear in identical form for the parents and the children; by getting answers to them for each generation it can be seen if there is any definite change from one generation to the next. The scholarship question is interesting from that point of view and also for quite another purpose. Does order in the family have anything to do with mental ability? Is the seventh child of a seventh child, as one saying has it, more apt than others to be a genius, or do the bright boys and girls come just as readily or more readily among the first-born or the second? If, after allowing for all differences of economic or educational conditions, we could answer those questions with assurance, we should have established a scientific fact of real importance. We might do that, if we can get enough answers.

This is explained more fully in the next chapter on "Nature and Nurture." Here I am concerned with the simpler vital side of the family—with the number of children born and when they were born. What do we hope to learn from this part of the form?

Let me name, first, though it is rather technical, one point on which further knowledge is badly needed, and will be given if the form gets filled in sufficiently.

That the age of the parents has some effect on the prospect of their having children is obvious.

Precisely what that effect is in Britain we do not know. In other countries, when a birth is registered, the ages of the parents must be stated; here they are not stated; we do not, therefore, know directly the relation between age of parents and size of family. Yet for some purposes, in the scientific study of population problems, it is indispensable to know this relation or to estimate it. Such an authority as Sir Arthur Newsholme, in writing of the British birth-rate, for want of satisfactory British figures had to assume that figures derived from Sweden were applicable to the British population, and I have followed him. Of course, there is no real justification for that assumption, though it was the best that we could do. We ought to make our own statistics on such a point, not have to import them.

This point about the relation between age of parents and prospect of children, though important, is rather technical. Let me turn to something that is both important and something that everybody can understand.

There is one general result of our family census that can be foretold in advance. The families born of the later marriages will, on the whole, be markedly smaller in size. The birth-rate has been falling; the later families will have fewer children. That is the most important single fact that is certain to emerge and must dominate all our thinking about the future of the family and of our population.

The theory of population which ruled a hundred

THE FAMILY AND POPULATION QUESTION

years ago treated human beings as liable to an indefinite increase, which could normally be held in check only by vice or misery. Man-power was like any other commodity; to pay more for it would only cause more to be produced, till the price fell again to the starvation costs of production. Under the imperious urge of sex, mankind could not escape the iron law of wages; all advances of prosperity would be destroyed by increase in numbers almost as soon as they were made.

That was the theory. The facts of population in the nineteenth century for a time put this theory out of court. Britain passed from being one of the richest agricultural countries of the world to being the richest industrial country, while her ten and a half millions of population became forty millions. As the population grew, wages grew also; the standard of living seemed able to rise indefinitely. But till fifty years ago it might have been argued that the day of pressure of population on subsistence was only being postponed by technical improvements and the development of international trade. Sooner or later the pressure would be felt. The population of Britain, as of most countries in Europe, still seemed destined for limitless increase, and it did not appear possible that subsistence would increase indefinitely to correspond.

Then came a change. In the midst of Britain's most rapidly rising prosperity, while incomes and wages and production and consumption and standard of living all went on swinging upwards, the birth-rate suddenly, about 1876, changed its course. From rising slowly, it began to fall and has continued to fall headlong. The number of children born for every thousand of the population, the crude "birth-rate," as it is called by statisticians, was 36·3 in 1876. In 1931 it was 15·8. For every thousand married women of an age to have children, more than three hundred children were actually born fifty years ago; less than one hundred and thirty are born now. The total number of births to-day is barely two-thirds of what it was thirty years ago.

The change in the course of the birth-rate with the course of marriages and of real income is shown in Chart II.[1] The birth-rate, based on the numbers of married women between fifteen and forty-five years of age, shows a slow rise to 1876, followed by a rapid fall, whose course is broken only by the disturbance of the war, bringing few births from 1917 to 1919, and very many in 1920.

The marriage rate, based on the numbers of marriageable men, shows before the war a fluctuation in accordance with the state of trade and employment; it shows, in 1914 and just after the war, in 1919 and 1920, marriage booms having little immediate effect on births. Apart from these points the outstanding feature of the marriage curve is a marked drop of general level between

[1] The chart and figures represented are taken from an article by myself on "The Fall of Fertility Among European Races," brought up to date (*Economica*, March 1925)."

THE FAMILY AND POPULATION QUESTION

CHART II

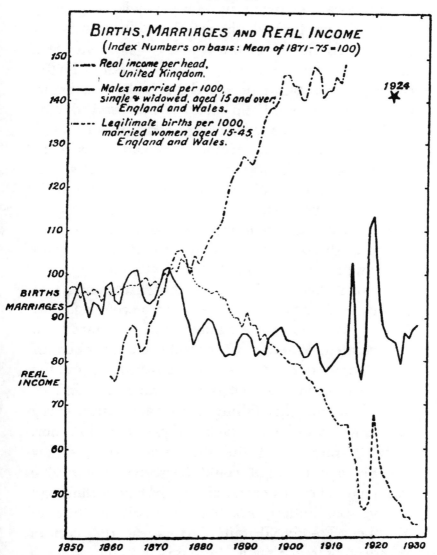

1875 and 1880—that is to say, at the time when the birth-rate changed its course; this suggests a common cause for both changes then. The marriage-rate also continues on the whole to fall from 1880 till the war. Since the war, though the fall of births continues, the trend of marriage looks like being upwards; this trend, however, is not marked and might be due to changes of age constitution.

The curve of real income per head, that is to say of income allowing for the estimated changes in the cost of living, rises steadily from its beginning in 1860 to about 1900, showing no change of economic conditions to account for the change in the course of the birth-rate and the simultaneous drop in the marriage-rate about 1876.

There is here a change in the fundamentals of society with no obvious cause to account for it. The importance of the change itself can hardly be exaggerated. Whether we consider the numbers of total population, or its age constitution, or the change in economic demand, or the size of individual families, the falling birth-rate alters every problem. Let us look at each of those points in order.

As to number of the total population, a few decades ago no limit could be seen; only twelve years ago a famous economist again raised the bogy of over-population, not only in Britain, but in Europe. To-day Britain has a nearly certain prospect of reaching a stationary population in a few years, and a good chance of a declining population. Nearly all other nations of European stock, in Europe or outside, seem to be moving, more or less rapidly, to the same goal as Britain.

Next as to age constitution. By the age constitution of a population is meant the proportions in it of people of various ages. In a population that is growing rapidly, there are proportionately more young people. In one that is stationary there are proportionately more old ones. An increasing population has more idle mouths of children to maintain, but grows continually stronger to maintain them as each larger generation reaches manhood; that is the reign of youth. A stationary population has more idle mouths of pensioners at the other end of life; it has proportionately more middle-aged and ageing minds in charge of its affairs. Those who listened to Dr. Haldane's talk on Science and Civilisation and the ages of the British Cabinet[1] will appreciate the point of this.

As to changes in economic demand, growth of the demand for the essentials of life in food and shelter depends on growth of population far more directly than does the demand for comforts and luxuries. The same number of men can learn to enjoy more luxuries—to buy gramophones or bicycles, to visit more cinemas or to travel more—as scientific improvements bring these things within their reach. But they cannot eat much more of the essential foods; the human stomach is limited. One

[1] Printed in the *Listener*, February 3rd, 1932.

of the reasons for over-production and distress among farmers to-day is probably that great technical advance in the methods of agriculture has coincided with a decline in the growth of population.

As to the individual family, let me put the fall of the birth-rate in a new way. Out of every three married women under forty-five years of age in 1876, one had a child born in the course of that year and two did not. Out of every eight married women under forty-five years of age in 1930, one had a child in that year and seven out of eight did not. If we think of the time before birth and after birth and the numbers who had no children at all, the 1876 proportion makes wifehood for all the rest almost continuous motherhood; the proportion was actually just less than one in three, but near enough for practical purposes. What a difference the 1930 proportion of one in eight must mean—in the occupation of married women! It is far more important than any change of legal status.

The fall of the birth-rate, of course, has been offset in part by a fall of the death-rate, most directly by a decline of infant mortality. Of 1,000 children born alive in Britain a generation ago, more than 150 died within a year. Of the same number born to-day about 70 die in the first year.

The fall of the birth-rate, nevertheless, in Britain, Europe, America, Australia, wherever the European races have spread, remains one of the most important events of the past century. With all that lies behind

THE FAMILY AND POPULATION QUESTION 49

it and all that it may portend, I am inclined to reckon it a turning-point in human history.

To understand it is of overwhelming importance. To understand it, we need far more knowledge than now we have. Families on the average are smaller than they were, but we have learned to distrust general averages. How is the decline distributed by occupations and how related to economic conditions, such as the employment of married women? Again, with families of a later generation smaller as a whole than those of earlier generations, does this happen because children do not come so soon after marriage, or stop coming sooner, or come at longer intervals? What differences in the upbringing of children and their relations to one another arise through there being fewer of them? On all such questions and many more, on all the varied effects of the falling birth-rate, our investigation will, it is hoped, throw light, will show the falling birth-rate, not as a figure in a blue-book, but as it works out in the lives of innumerable families.

These effects of the falling birth-rate are important. Even more important for study are the causes of the fall; on knowing causes depends any forecast of the future. In one sense the main cause is clear; men and women generally have come to take thought about the birth of children and the size of their families, as they did not take thought sixty or seventy years ago. But what motives have led them to this course, what motives might influence them differently in future, all that is implied in this change for the relations of the sexes—to such questions the answers are not known. Nor can we say that there are not other causes also for the falling birth-rate—causes beyond human influence.

With this question of causes, of why families to-day are so much smaller than they used to be, the Family Form itself is not directly concerned. The question involves analysis of human motives and raises issues of human conduct on which opinion differs strongly. To throw light on it, information is needed of a type that could hardly be asked for in a form intended for broadcast distribution. But information furnished by individuals voluntarily about themselves is needed here as much as on other sides of family life. Anyone who is prepared to give such further information, as to factors affecting the size of the family, is invited to mark the Family Form with a cross in the appropriate place in section L; he will, in due course, receive a further communication from the School of Economics. It is hoped that many will do so, however their views may differ as to what it is right or wrong for human beings to do in seeking to limit their families. On this vital issue the views of people of all shades of opinion are needed. For the size of families is one of the central problems of nearly all civilised societies to-day.

III

NATURE AND NURTURE

STRICTLY, this chapter is not about the family, though it is about things which we can only learn of through the family, and by the help of families. It is about what human beings are and what makes them as they are. All men are made partly by Nature and partly by Nurture.

The nature of each individual is what he inherits physically from his father and mother, all the potentialities that lie ready to develop in the invisible cell, derived from both parents, with which each human being begins. For each individual his nature is fixed, when he begins; is fixed, not at birth, but some nine months before. The Chinese, with that rather perverse logic which is typical of them, reckon each person's age from that moment, and not from his birth, so that every Chinaman, according to our standards, is some nine months younger than he calls himself.

Nurture, in the narrow sense, means feeding. In the sense in which I use it here, to contrast with nature, it means environment. Nurture is the whole perpetually changing environment in which, from the moment that the human being becomes an individual, that human being is surrounded, and in response to which the potentialities hidden in his nature are developed or stunted, turned this way or that way. Nurture is what he eats and wears and is taught, where he lives and whom he meets. Nurture begins, of course, before birth; it continues through life to play upon the individual.

Nature is fixed in each individual. In the race it is not fixed; it can be changed, but substantially it can be changed in one way only—by selective breeding. Everybody is familiar with deliberate selective breeding among animals and plants. By choosing the right parents, cart-horses can be bred for strength, race-horses for speed, cattle for meat or milk, wheat for power to resist disease, roses for colour or scent. By choosing, in each generation, those who show some marked characteristic, to be the parents of the next generation, that particular characteristic can as a rule be made more prominent, can be developed. Equally some particular characteristic, if it is thought undesirable, can as a rule be bred out of the stock by choosing as the parents only those who are without it.

The limiting words in those last two statements are important; the words, "as a rule." Not all characteristics can be affected by selective beeding, can be bred in or bred out; that can be done only if they are inheritable. Some things can be inherited and others cannot; broadly, anything that one acquires in going through life cannot be passed on directly to one's son—whether it is a broken nose or a knowledge of Greek—though a tendency to acquire such things may be passed on, such as irritability making it more likely that one will get into a fight, or mental ability of the kind that makes learning languages easy.

To find out exactly what can be inherited and what cannot be inherited is the first problem in social biology. But behind that are many other problems, for heredity is a complex affair, and inheritable characters differ from one another in many ways. Some are common, like straight hair, and some are very rare, like a white forelock or albinism. Some are dominant—that is to say, may show themselves though derived through one parent only; others are recessive—that is to say, show themselves only if they can be traced in the stocks from which both parents come. Recessive characters may be passed on as unseen potentialities through one parent from one generation to another, ready to show themselves as soon as they meet with the same latent potentiality in the other partner to a mating. Red hair or blue eyes are common instances of recessive characters. Some characters, again, are linked in one way or another with sex—that is to say, are passed on differently by the father and the mother respectively. Colour-blindness is one of these.

Inheritance alike in man and in animals and plants is complex. In essentials it is the same for all. Selective breeding could, in theory, be applied to human beings as it is applied to animals or plants.

If in some imaginary society the right to mate and bring up children were reserved for people under five feet six inches high, the average stature of people in that society would gradually diminish. In practice, selective breeding by design has not been applied to human beings and would be hard to apply. But it does not follow that selective breeding without design may not be taking place. The laws and customs of a particular community may be such as, without our desire and perhaps without our knowledge, to favour the development of particular inheritable characters and discourage the development of others. The institutions of any community at any time can hardly avoid making marriage and the rearing of children easier for one section than another. The enforced celibacy of the priesthood, for instance, or, later, the restrictions on the marriage of teachers in our ancient Universities, must both have tended to diminish certain qualities in the stock. Behind our backs, unconscious selective breeding is at work, changing the nature of our stock, improving it perhaps for some purposes and making it worse for other purposes, developing immunity from some diseases and not from others. Nature is powerful in us, but can slowly be changed by breeding and is changed continuously.

Nurture also is very powerful. Though it cannot directly affect the race, it can make surprising differences in individuals. The queen bee is a familiar instance; by nature she is one, any one, of the many thousand barren females in the hive; by special feeding and housing at the right moment one larva, that, with ordinary nurture, would have become a barren worker, is turned into a queen, able to be the mother of the whole of the next generation. A less familiar but even stranger transformation can be caused by nurture in tadpoles. If they are brought up, as most tadpoles are, in muddy water, they have two eyes, one on each side of the head. If they are transferred at a certain stage to a solution of alcohol, they grow one eye only, on the top of the head; whether that single eye nurtured on alcohol sees double or not, science does not relate.

Let me give one more illustration of the power of Nurture, somewhat nearer (I hope) to the interests and experience of most of us, than becoming one-eyed through excess of alcohol. In America, adoption is a good deal commoner than in this country, and makes it possible to compare children of different parents in the same home. It seems there to have been established that children of different parentage who have been brought up from infancy in the same home, though less like one another than children of the same parents, are intellectually much more like one another than children of different parents in different homes.

But the environment which thus works directly on individuals cannot fail at the same time to work indirectly on Nature in the race. What may be good in Nurture may be bad for Nature, and *vice versa*.

It is just because of this that it becomes of such fundamental importance to know what in human beings is due to Nature and what to Nurture. That is perhaps the most crucial problem in all social science, and it is one of the hardest to solve. In the case of animals we can experiment both in breeding and in feeding. With human beings we cannot experiment. We cannot, for instance, arrange, as someone suggested, that a large number of families should adopt one another's second and subsequent children at birth, so that in family A would be one child of heredity A and others of heredity B, C, etc., while in family B would be children of heredity B, C, A, and so on. That would be a most illuminating experiment, but is made impossible by the natural preference of parents for their own children. Occasionally, however, children do get adopted when very young by families with other children and thus give the chance, by appropriate measurement, to compare the effects of Nurture and Nature. That is one of the experiments which unconsciously human beings sometimes make for the benefit of social science.

Broadly, in social science, we cannot experiment deliberately; we have to rely upon the occasional experiments which human beings or Nature make for us. The rest of this chapter describes some of those experiments.

First may be mentioned marriages of cousins and other near relations. I am not concerned here to say whether such marriages are good or bad. Some people have a prejudice against them; other people favour them. I do not myself believe that science is in a position to pass general judgment either way, and in this enquiry we are not seeking materials for such a judgment. The special interest of marriages between cousins is in the possibility of getting light on inheritable characters which are rare as well as recessive. A recessive character, as I have explained, though it may be passed on indefinitely, remains latent, until a mating occurs between people who both carry the latent potentiality for it. If the character itself is a rare one, it may be many generations before two people of different stocks each carrying this potentiality meet and mate. The character will not show itself unless it is in the stock of both parents; the chance of this, of course, is much greater if the parents themselves have a common ancestor. It is, therefore, to marriages between people of common ancestry that most of our knowledge of rare recessive characters, such as albinism, in human beings is due. It is largely to such marriages that we must look for more knowledge. That is why we ask in the Family Form if the marriage described there is a marriage of cousins or of people otherwise related or not. If people who are so married will help us, we shall probably ask them to tell us a little more about themselves, though, of course, they need not, if they do not want to. I should add that by an oversight in the form we have not asked those who fill in section B to tell us if their parents in section G were related. Naturally we should like to know of such cases.

Second may be mentioned the occasional experiment which Nature makes for us by bringing about the birth of twins. An experiment means trial, and possibly twins are occasionally a trial to their parents. On the whole, most people regard them as a very attractive experiment by Nature. How many people, however, realize that there are two quite different sorts of twins? Most of us, perhaps, have been struck by the fact that sometimes twins do not seem particularly like one another, and that other twins are as like as two peas. In fact, those two sorts of twins are quite distinct and come about by different natural processes. The twins that are not particularly like one another are in a sense accidentally twins, they are two children of the same father and mother who happen to be born at the same time. They have a certain common heredity, but they have nothing more in common than ordinary brothers and sisters born with intervals between them; one may be tall and one short, one a boy and one a girl, one with red hair and one with black. If they do grow up more like one another than other brothers and sisters, that is because, coming at the same time, they are more likely to get the same Nurture.

Contrasted with these accidental twins are the identical twins. They have not been separate from the beginning; they started life together in the same cell, which then divided. They are invariably of the same sex, both boys or both girls. They are as like as two peas, far more like than ordinary brothers or sisters or accidental twins. Their mothers often cannot distinguish them. Their identity extends to such highly individualized things as finger-prints.[1] They have, in fact, the same nature. Every difference between them must be a difference of nurture. They give one of the best chances we have of disentangling Nature and Nurture.[2]

If identical twins could be separated at birth, anything common to them would be either heredity or the result of Nurture limited to the nine months before birth.

If, therefore, one can find a pair of identical twins who have not been brought up together, they are enormously well worth studying. At about four births in every 350 births in Britain there are twins: of these four pairs, one is identical and three are accidental. This means that in the next five years about nine thousand pairs of identical twins will be born in Britain. If one of each of fifty such pairs could be adopted at birth by a different family,

[1] A lady who heard this talk gave me as an illustration of similarity between identical twins the case of her two sons who at school were made to share equally all punishments incurred by either, because the masters could not distinguish them.
[2] This account of identical and other twins is based mainly on a chapter in *Genetic Principles in Medicine and Social Science* by L. T. Hogben, Professor of Social Biology in the University of London (1931).

and brought up differently, and the two could be watched and compared as they grew up, the science of social biology would make a leap forward. We cannot do that kind of experiment, but by learning more about twins without interfering with family life we can still hope to learn a great deal. That is why we ask specially about twins in the Family Form. Asking people to give us information on a form is not interfering with the Family. It is the alternative to interfering or to blank ignorance about vital problems.

Cousin marriages are very rare,[1] and twins are not very common. Let me come to something that concerns every family, on which every family can help us. All children are born in a certain order and at certain ages of their parents. What difference, if any, does it make to be first-born or second, or last —to be born when one's parents are quite young or when they are older? If it does make any difference the difference almost certainly represents Nurture rather than Nature.

The Nature that each individual transmits to his children, though not the same for each child, does not vary in any definite direction through life. The differences of Nature between children of the same two parents depend upon the different ways in which what they derive from their two parents blends at the beginning. So far as we can judge, the blending

[1] This is not true of all peoples. Sir George Grierson has pointed out to me that in Muhammadan countries, and especially in Arabia, such marriages are common and highly approved, and that they are common also among English Gypsies.

is by chance, with little, if any, bias through the age of the parents or the order of birth. If, therefore, there is any point in which later children *as such* differ from earlier children, the difference cannot be due to Nature; it is due to Nurture. If there is any factor that shows itself more commonly with later children than with earlier ones, it is to some extent at least a factor due to Nurture—to difference of feeding and surroundings, before birth or after.

Any particular feature, indeed, may be both inheritable to some extent and to some extent a product of Nurture. The tendency to have twins, for instance, is probably to some extent hereditary; that is to say, people of certain stocks are probably more likely to have twins than other people. But the birth of twins is also associated with a particular age of the mother; a larger proportion of all births between the ages of thirty-five and forty are twin births than at any other period of life. Next to that, twins come most commonly after forty; Thackeray was quite a good social biologist in bringing the Newcome twins into the world, rather unexpectedly, when their mother was forty-three.[1]

[1] The Castlewood twins seem to have been born much earlier in their mother's life. Whether they were identical or not is an interesting question. They were exceedingly like one another, but their hair, at least in early childhood, was of different shades. The Newcome twins were upset from a go-cart in their infancy by their elder brother Tom Newcome, and the mark left on the nose of Brian enabled Tom Newcome in later life at once to distinguish them. This suggests that they were identical.

Mental deficiency and special mental ability alike furnish other instances of qualities to some extent inheritable and to some extent due to Nurture. Some kinds of deficiency are clearly inheritable. Other kinds seem to be connected with the age of the mother or order of birth, to afflict more commonly than others, persons born late in their mother's life or at the end of a large family. The first kind could be eliminated or diminished only by breeding out. The second kind could be diminished, though not eliminated altogether, if fewer children were born after their mother was thirty-five.[1]

The case of special mental ability raises a question of more general interest. That such ability is to some extent inheritable seems clear. To what extent, however, can it also be developed by appropriate Nurture, as the queen bee can be developed from any ordinary worker? That is one of the points of our scholarship question. Of course, one cannot judge mental ability of all kinds simply by scholarships; some children get specially trained to win scholarships and others do not; some children develop early, others develop late. Of course, also one must allow for changes in the scholarship system itself. But with care this should be possible. If it is possible, and if we do find in our returns any tendency either way, it does not matter which way, if scholarship children tend to come more

[1] Mongolism seems to be a deficiency of this second kind (*see* Hogben, *op. cit.*, Ch. IV, and particularly p. 103).

commonly either early in the family or late in the family, then we shall establish something both interesting and important. To the extent that we find such a tendency we shall be bound to say that the winning of scholarships depends upon Nurture, because order in family is the sign of Nurture rather than of Nature.

In the preceding chapter I mentioned the old saying about the seventh child of a seventh child being a genius. Of course, I did not mean that particular saying to be taken too seriously. If it were all true, it would be most surprising. For in so far as a person shows special ability because he is a seventh child, his ability presumably arises through Nurture not Nature, and he could not transmit that to his children. The seventh child may tend to be cleverer than those born before him; but it would upset everything we think we know of heredity to find that the seventh child of a seventh child tends to be any cleverer than the seventh child of a first-born.

In this chapter we are not concerned with old sayings or with any definite view at all. I am not even going to suggest whether on the whole I expect in the returns to find the late children cleverer than the early ones, or the other way round, or no difference either way. In particular families it sometimes goes one way and sometimes the other. What we want to find out is whether, if one takes enough families, one gets in the end any definite tendency either way.

Order in family is, indeed, one of the most generally interesting things to study, one of the most hopeful avenues of progress in social biology. If we get the number of forms that we now seem likely to get, we shall have an unparalleled collection of facts showing order in family, and enabling us to relate that to all sorts of other characteristics, to sex, to viability (that is, length of life), to fertility (that is, number of children) as well as to scholarships. We might get some astonishingly interesting as well as important results. Anything that can be associated with order at birth, *anything*—physique, mental ability, fertility, viability, anything—is to the extent of the association presumably due to Nurture and not to Nature. Anything due to Nurture can be changed, if it wants changing, or developed, if it wants developing, by changing or developing the Nurture. Of course, changing the Nurture is not always a simple process. Nurture means what happens in the nine months before birth as well as what happens after. But if we can find out just where the Nurture comes in that is producing either a good or a bad result, we can encourage it or change it if we will.

To know what is due to Nurture is to know what we can change directly. To know what is due to Nature is to know what we cannot change directly, what we must accept for ever, unless we are prepared to influence the breeding of our stock.

To contribute anything, therefore, to the disentangling of Nature and Nurture in human kind is so important that in itself it would justify the whole of our enquiry. The kind of contribution we can hope to make to that depends essentially on the number of forms that we receive. How many people care to tell us about the economic or social sides of family life—how family income is managed or jobs are obtained—is less important. How many people give us on the first two pages and later the simple vital facts of births and deaths, ages and marriages in their own households and those of their parents, is all-important. The larger the number of forms, the more certain and more searching can we make our statistical analysis, our search for correlations.

In such statistical analysis all depends on numbers just as in astronomy some things depend on the size of the telescope. To promote astronomical science the Rockefeller Foundation are just establishing, in the best astronomical climate in the world, the largest telescope in the world, on Mount Wilson in California, with new magnifying power—to bring in the new heavens, an instrument to show countless stars and nebulae too small or too far away to have been seen before, an instrument to separate things confused before, to measure their relations and their distances, to see how the dead universe is made. This family investigation by the B.B.C., for all the nonsense that has been talked about it and against it by some people, is a sober attempt to see if with the help of listeners we can construct a new kind of instrument for social science, an instrument of power to discover subtle relations hitherto unseen and to reveal how living humanity is made. Every single additional form filled up in those vital sections A, B, and D, even if nowhere else, is an addition to the power of that instrument, to our hope of new discoveries.

IV

THE ECONOMICS OF FAMILY LIFE

Discussion between Dr. Hugh Dalton (*H.D.*)
and Mrs. Eleanor Barton (*E.B.*)

E.B. A large number of the problems of Family Life resolve themselves into questions of economics, and the answer to many, if not most, of them is, "Can I afford it?" The fall in the birth-rate, for example, is a question which is inseparable from economic motive. And in the economics of family life women have an important part to play. Not only are they responsible for spending most of the family income, but there must be thousands of women—tens of thousands rather—who after marriage have some paid work outside their home and thus contribute directly to the family exchequer.

H.D. Yes, indeed. According to the census of 1921, there were nearly seven hundred thousand married women working outside their homes in England and Wales and more than forty thousand in Scotland. That means, for the country as a whole, one married woman in every eleven under sixty-five years of age. In addition there were nearly half a million widows under sixty-five working—more than one in every four. But a great many of these will have been war widows, or may have re-married by now, or given up outside work.

E.B. It would be interesting to see how those figures for 1921 compare with the census of last year.

H.D. Yes, the corresponding figures for the 1931 census aren't published yet. Between 1911 and 1921 it appears that the percentage of married women working outside the home fell slightly, though the total number increased a little owing to the growth of the population.

But, if you go back not ten years, but a century or two, you get a very different picture. Factories and offices are quite modern inventions. A hundred and fifty years ago women had no opportunity for working in such places, even if they wanted to. And go back still further to quite early stages of human history. There you find that, while the men went out hunting and fishing, the women used to do all the heavy drudgery. In some parts of Africa to-day this is still the rule. With the progress of what we call Civilisation many things change—and the idea that the husband alone ought to support his family out of his earnings is comparatively modern. Before the days of factories the home was often the workshop; women and children worked along with the men, and the products of their joint labour in the home were sold through middle-men. Perhaps you remember Defoe's vivid description of the home workshops of the Yorkshire cloth-makers in the early eighteenth century. Those women and children were earning money for the support of the family, but they earned it inside the home.

E.B. And of course women used to *make* many things inside the home which are now generally made outside it—bread, jams and pickles, butter, cheese, and so on. And then the clothes of the family were generally made at home.

H.D. Yes, of course, they were contributing to the support of the family in that way. But the Industrial Revolution led to the gradual break-up of the home as a workshop. This breaking-up process has been going on steadily ever since. The principle of the division of labour has been pushed farther and farther. The present tendency is to do more and more by communal arrangements outside the home, rather than by family arrangements inside it. There is less washing done at home, and more at laundries. There is much less bread baked at home than there used to be. There is even less cooking done in the home than there used to be, and more at canteens and popular restaurants.

E.B. But many wives still make their own bread in the North, you know. And although eating in restaurants may be common in London, you don't find it so much in the provinces. Of course I am not denying that even in the North we do buy food prepared ready to eat. In Lancashire, where there is so much married women's labour, the fish-and-chip shops do a roaring supper trade.

H.D. Yes, that's true. But I might give other

examples which would apply to the North and Midlands more than the South—the development of pithead baths in some of the coal-mining districts, for instance. In any case, the effect of these modern developments is that married women have had to seek opportunities of earning outside the home. Since they couldn't contribute to the support of the family in the old way, they had to look for new ways of doing it. There's no change in principle involved.

E.B. But there's still a good deal of prejudice against married women's work—prejudice, I'm sorry to say, which attaches particularly to better-paid jobs and to work in which women come into competition with men.

H.D. Yes, but don't you think that that prejudice, at any rate in some of the professions, has been dying down since the war? You have women barristers now, as well as women doctors, and women architects, and women members of the House of Commons and of the Government. Of course, the House of Lords is still purely a men's club and women, whether married or single, aren't yet allowed to become bishops or ambassadors.

E.B. But my point is that there's no objection to married women doing charring, cleaning, scrubbing, cooking, and drudging house-work.

H.D. In fact, to all those occupations which are generally considered to be "women's work."

E.B. I've never heard objections raised to the work

done by that army of women who cross the river night and morning to clean London's offices and buildings in the City and West End.

I should feel better disposed towards those who objected to married women's work, if they objected to this kind of drudgery too. It seems to me that we've got to reorganise our ideas of women's work in the home. For the most part it's been hard, laborious, unpaid work done uncomplainingly. The man who boasts that he's always kept his wife at home without working has forgotten that the washing of his shirts and socks, the cleaning of his house and the cooking of his meals, *is* work, and has to be paid for when done outside the home. But it's against married women in professional jobs that most prejudice is felt.

H.D. Yes, I admit the prejudice, but it's not confined to men.

E.B. I know that well enough. But tell me, if a married woman is specially qualified to do a piece of work, why on earth should she not be allowed to do it if she wants to? Why should you differentiate between married women and single women any more than between married men and single men? Oh, I know the answer is Economics. But quite apart from the economic necessity which drives a large number of married women to work, there is the fact that married women are finding their work in the home is growing less and less, the increase of labour-saving devices, the habit of living in flats and small houses, fewer children in the family, and so on, all have their effect. Moreover, nowadays a woman is not content to spend her time polishing this and rubbing that—her household gods are not brass candlesticks and steel fire-irons. She wants, and is beginning to get, things like stainless steel, gas cooking and heating, electric lighting, vacuum-cleaners, and so on. So a married woman is at liberty to seek a more serious, or at any rate a different kind of, occupation. Increasing numbers of women will want to express themselves outside the home. Then there is the decrease in the birth-rate which is altering the old idea that a married woman's job is simply to bring children into the world. She will not care for the children less because there are fewer of them; rather she will put forward greater efforts to give them opportunities which were denied to her. In section E of the Family Form married women at work are being asked to give their reason for working. I wonder how many of them will say that they earn money in order to provide for the education and care of their children—to give them the advantages of a secondary education or some special training or apprenticeship. And there's a curious paradox here, because I know that a large number of mothers work in order to be able to give their children better chances than they had, yet at the same time the very fact that these mothers have to go out to work prevents them from having more children. It would be very interesting to know how many mothers would like to have had more children, if only they could have been assured of the means of bringing them up properly and giving them a good start in life.

H.D. Yes, and it would be interesting to know how many marriages are childless because the wife is at work. Of course, you know, Mrs. Barton, some people still say that a married woman's first duty is to stay at home and look after her children, and that, if she hasn't got any children, she ought to have. I remember a famous professor at Cambridge who, when someone had suggested giving votes to women, said, "Don't give them votes, teach them to be mothers."

E.B. Oh yes, I know that argument. It's not only held by professors at Cambridge.

H.D. Well, it's an argument which may appeal at the present time to those who think it dangerous that our national birth-rate should have sunk so low, and fear that in days to come the world will be overrun by more prolific races like the Russians or the Japanese or the native races of Africa. Then there's another argument which is often used against married women's work—that the competition of married women in the labour market brings down men's wages, and that, if the women would only stay at home, the men would be able to earn more.

E.B. I know, and it's also said that a man should receive a living wage, sufficient to bring up his family in reasonable comfort, without his wife having to go out and work for wages as well as himself.

H.D. And, of course, you will have heard it said that the presence of so many married women in the labour market causes a lot of unemployment among the men.

E.B. Oh yes, I know. It's said that the women take away the men's jobs. . . .

H.D. And that the employers prefer the women because they are cheaper than men and also because they're not such good trade unionists. Well, people may disagree as to whether married women *ought* to go out to work. But the fact remains that they *do* go out to work in very large numbers. There are some extraordinary variations, though, between different parts of the country. In London, the percentage of married women working, according to the census of 1921, was 13. That's a little above the average for the country as a whole. But the percentage was over 42 in Burnley and much the same in Blackburn. It was 22 in Stoke-on-Trent, and 19 in Bradford. On the other hand, it was under 5 in Wiltshire, and about 3 in Aberdeen, and in the administrative county of Durham, apart from the County Boroughs, it was actually less than 2 per cent. Of course the reason for these variations is to be found in the industrial character of different districts. In many parts of the country we have allowed one particular industry to dominate the means of livelihood of the whole district. This is a great weakness in our

THE ECONOMICS OF FAMILY LIFE

economic organisation, as recent experience shows. In some districts we have put all our industrial eggs in one basket, and if the bottom falls out of that basket, the district is smitten with wholesale unemployment and distress.

The result of this excessive local specialization is that in some areas there are practically no opportunities for work by women outside the home. A predominantly mining area like County Durham is an example, and the opportunities are not much better in the iron and steel and shipbuilding centres like Middlesbrough or Sunderland, nor in the mainly agricultural counties like Wiltshire, nor in a mixed agricultural and fishing county like Aberdeen. London, on the other hand, with its great local concentration of wealth and population, and its great variety of occupations and enterprise, offers many openings for women's work. But the employment of married women is at a maximum in the cotton towns of Lancashire, and it's much above the average in a wool textile centre like Bradford, or a pottery centre like Stoke.

There's another interesting point about these figures, and that is the relationship which they bear to the birth-rate in the various areas. Everyone knows that the birth-rate in the coal-mining districts is high and in cotton districts it is low. In County Durham the birth-rate now is 21 per thousand of the population, but in Blackburn it is only 12·8, whereas the average for the country as a whole is 16·3.

CHART III

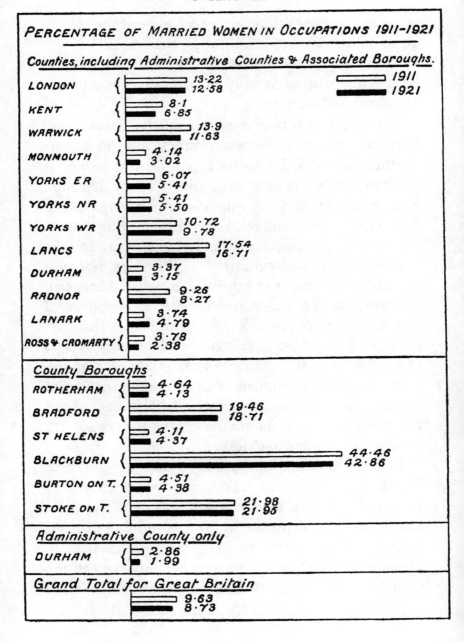

No doubt there are many reasons for these variations, but one obvious reason is that the number of children which a married woman cotton operative can have depends upon the amount of time she can spare from her work, and on the arrangements she can make for the care of her children while she is out working.

E.B. Yes, I remember the old days in Lancashire when women had to go out to work at six o'clock in the morning. The mother used to take the child from its warm bed, wrap it in a shawl, and take it out in the raw cold morning to an old granny, who took care of it till the mother called for it again on her return in the evening. And then in the evening there was all the household work to do, cooking, cleaning, and so on. It's not so bad now, but it's far from satisfactory. Yet it's still the case in many working-class homes that the elder children have to look after the younger while the mother is at work. Believe me, the old-fashioned "little mother" has by no means disappeared from working-class homes. I have heard this favourably commended as one means of teaching the child to be domestic and helpful, but I have never been able to see any good come from placing these heavy burdens of responsibility on such young shoulders. Happily there are fewer children in a family nowadays, and from all accounts they are stronger and healthier.

H.D. I should say that a great deal of this improvement has been brought about by the State and the

Municipality, through the development of public health and educational services.

E.B. Yes, I'm sure that children's welfare centres and maternity clinics and other social services of that character have been of immense value to working-class mothers. And then nursery schools. I'd like to see nursery schools in every town and village in this country. It is only the less thoughtful mothers who still prefer to keep their babies at home even under slum conditions. But it's only stupidity or sentimentality which puts any case for keeping the children always at home, unless the home conditions are of the best. And there will still be plenty for the mother to do for her child, even if the State takes over the care of its health and education.

H.D. I see, Mrs. Barton, that we agree that the State should do a great deal more for the family. I take it from what you say that you do not regard children as being the exclusive possession of their parents.

E.B. I certainly don't. Some years ago I was speaking at a conference in favour of a resolution to keep children at school until they were fifteen years old at least. In fact, I said I would prefer sixteen. One of the delegates in opposing the resolution put forward this argument, "Why, if they're kept at school until they're sixteen, then they'll be getting married, and you'll get nowt out of 'em." Still that was many years ago, and things have changed, and although many people still feel that an extra year or two years at school is a luxury we ought not to contemplate, I know many parents are anxious to see the school-leaving age raised, and would be glad to see it raised, even though it meant additional economic burdens for them.

H.D. Yes, I'm sure that's true of many parents. It used to be said that children were often regarded simply as little economic assets. But legal restrictions on the employment of children, and the raising of the school-leaving age even up to the present limit of fourteen, have done a good deal to alter that. Of course, in the long run the children may be even greater assets to their parents, if they are prevented from starting work too soon, and are given a better education. And certainly they should be greater assets to themselves and to the community. But you will remember, Mrs. Barton, that when it was proposed to raise the school-leaving age to fifteen, it was also proposed to pay maintenance allowances to the parents during the extra year. And some have gone farther and proposed that children's allowances should be paid to mothers from the birth of their children until they left school and started earning. That suggestion has interested me a good deal. It would, of course, be a big extension of the principle of State provision for the needs of the family.

E.B. I expect you have found, as I have, that there are great differences of opinion as to whether these suggested family allowances are good or not. Many people are against the idea.

H.D. Yes, some are against it because they think it will undermine the responsibility of the parents, and some are in favour of it because they think it will redistribute part of the income of the country more in accordance with family needs. And some are in favour of the principle, but would like the additional provision for the children to be given not in money but in kind. And some say the country can't afford it. . . .

E.B. And others say that we can afford it much better than some of the things on which we spend money at present—on armaments, for example.

H.D. And some say that the bachelors ought to pay for it by taxes on their beer and baccy and other luxuries which the man with a family can't afford.

E.B. And some trade unionists are against it because they think it would lead to a reduction in wages.

H.D. And other trade unionists are in favour of it because they think it would increase the union's bargaining power. There is a State scheme on a small scale actually in operation in New Zealand at the present time. And perhaps it would interest you to know, Mrs. Barton, that at the London School of Economics we have been paying children's allowances to members of the staff for several years, and the scheme has been working quite satisfactorily.

E.B. Well, perhaps in ten or fifteen years you will be able to answer questions like these:

Has the number of married persons on the staff of the School of Economics increased? Has the number of children per family increased? Have the authorities of the school preferred bachelors to married men in making new appointments—or have they preferred single women?

It seems to me that one can't make up one's mind about family allowances until one has definite answers to questions like these.

H.D. Quite true. The experience of the School of Economics and of countries like New Zealand may help us in due course to answer such questions.

E.B. This question of family allowances brings one up against old-age pensions. We can console ourselves that as a nation we give old-age pensions, but they're still far from adequate. The tragedy of old people is one of the worst aspects of our modern life. I should like to see special homes for old folk—homes where they can still have freedom and feel independent and where they would be given proper care and attention.

H.D. Personally I agree with what you say about the need for more generous old-age pensions, but it's important to remember that the number of old people is increasing and the number of children is diminishing. This fact has a bearing on the financial problem, for it means that the cost of any addition to the old-age pension scheme is bound to go up very fast as time goes on, but the cost of any additional provision you make for the children is likely to go down—whether that provision is by extended education or by family allowances or by increased medical services or in any other way. Any Chancellor of the Exchequer who is framing his Budget proposals will have to bear that difference in mind. As you probably know, quite apart from any national scheme, various pension schemes have been adopted in particular industries and occupations. Soldiers and sailors and airmen and policemen have their superannuation schemes. So have civil servants. So have teachers employed by local authorities. So have University teachers under the Federated Universities Scheme, which allows the teacher to move from one University to another and take his pension rights with him. A special scheme for miners, to be paid for by the various parties connected with the coal industry, has also been proposed, but I am sorry to say has not yet been adopted. Perhaps future advance in regard to old-age pensions will come by a multiplication of special schemes of this kind. I should like to see a compulsory retiring age for every occupation with adequate pensions for those who retire, so as to make more room for the younger generation, and give them a better chance of getting on.

E.B. Yes, if civil servants and teachers have a compulsory retiring age, why shouldn't miners and shop assistants?

H.D. Or even judges? And what a great reform it would be to apply the same rule to politicians!

E.B. I wonder how many of these changes we shall see during our lifetime?

V

THE FAMILY AS A SOCIAL GROUP

A Discussion between Sir William Beveridge (*W.B.*) and Professor Morris Ginsberg (*M.G.*)

W.B. I hope, Ginsberg, that in looking through the Family Form you noticed section J.

M.G. That is the section on meeting of partners, isn't it, Director? I certainly did notice it.

W.B. So did the newspapers. Some of the newspapers hardly noticed anything else. They had a tremendously good time with "Where did you meet your wife?" I don't grudge it to them. That one question probably got more press publicity for our scheme than anything else in the Family Form.

M.G. I have heard it suggested that that was the object of the question, to draw the Press.

W.B. No, really and truly, no. Of course, we thought that question might entertain listeners—might give them something pleasant and exciting to think back upon. There is no actual law against the b.b.c. giving listeners something pleasant to think about. But the question itself was not in any sense a joke or a stunt. Marriage is so important, both to the individual and to the community, that the way in which it comes about is also important. The degree to which chance or choice enters into the making of marriage, how far the choice of individuals is affected by the wills of others, what part is played by particular institutions, how the opportunities for meeting partners affect the mixing of different social classes, or the age of marriage—all these things are important. To try to learn about them isn't frivolous.

M.G. So Professor Seligman seems to think. He is, of course, one of the leading anthropologists in the country, and I was interested to see that in writing to the *Listener* a few weeks ago, he picked out this particular question as one of the most valuable and important in the Form.

W.B. I shouldn't put it as high as that myself. Of course, the way in which marriages come about is important, but we did not feel able, in a broadcast investigation, to ask for more than merely the place of first meeting. That may give some indication of tendencies, particularly if we can compare one generation with the next. But it can't give more than a very general indication. The place of first meeting, as my correspondents have pointed out, may not contribute anything material to the ultimate marriage. Quite a number of married people have assured me that they did not fall in love at first sight.

M.G. But if they had not met for the first time somewhere they would never have met. I hope that you will get enough answers for successive generations in section J to show tendencies. And, anyhow, I don't see how you could leave out of a Family Form all reference to the way in which marriages come about.

W.B. Do you think that the Family has a great deal to do with them?

M.G. Nowadays in England, of course, marriage is regarded as a purely personal matter for the two individuals. But I believe that a great many people, if they think back, will realize that their family circumstances had something to do with the matter—affected the age at which they married or the kind of person they married. In other times and other countries—indeed, for most of the human race for most of the time men have been on the earth—the family has had an enormously important part to play in regard to the marriages of its members. As far as the primitive peoples are concerned, we find that marriage is mostly an affair between the two families.

W.B. As it is with royalty. Nowadays even royalty is beginning to kick over the traces, but royal marriages used to be an important part of international diplomacy, a cause of peace and war.

M.G. To some extent the interest of the family in the marriages of its members among primitive peoples has the same basis. Many primitive tribes have rules requiring their members to marry outside the clan. The fact that a man must find a bride in another clan than his own helps to form links between different clans, and thus widens the area of peaceful co-operation. There are numerous peoples among whom the consent of the chief must be obtained for marriage. Indeed, sometimes the field of choice is narrowed, not only by excluding some marriages but also by positively insisting on others. In Australia, Melanesia, and Southern Asia there is a custom known as "cross-cousin marriage," according to which every man is expected to marry the daughter of his mother's brother, almost without question.

W.B. That must simplify very much a business which causes a deal of disturbance to some young people and their parents to-day. It is an improvement even on Dr. Johnson's plan.

M.G. What was that? I didn't know that Dr. Johnson was a sociologist.

W.B. Boswell asked him once if he didn't think that there were at least fifty women with whom a man could be just as happy as with the particular woman whom he had married. To this Johnson replied, "Ay, sir, fifty thousand," and he went on to suggest that marriages would in general be as happy, and often more so, if they were all made by the Lord Chancellor, upon a due consideration of the characters and circumstances, without the parties having any choice in the matter. What a gorgeous job of match-making for Lord Sankey!

M.G. Gilbert and Sullivan's Lord Chancellor in *Iolanthe* did something in that line. You'll remember, Director, that he used to "sit in Court all day, giving agreeable girls away."

W.B. He had only a handful of heiresses—wards

in Chancery—to hand out. Dr. Johnson's Lord Chancellor would have to work not only all day, but overtime, and on Sundays and Bank holidays, with a large staff. He'd be supposed to test their characters as well.

M.G. Well, to this day, probably over the greater part of the world, the family takes the place of the Lord Chancellor, and more or less directly arranges the marriages of its members.

W.B. Does the family give the parties no choice in the matter?

M.G. Some years ago Professor Hobhouse and I made a study of that very point. We found that in perhaps the larger number of cases the consent of the woman was not required, formally at least, though this differed, of course, with the stage of economic development. We found, for instance, that the consent of the woman was frequently not insisted upon among the pastoral peoples, while it was more respected among the agricultural peoples.

W.B. The girl grinding corn had more say than the milkmaid. I wonder why?

M.G. It depends really upon the stage of economic development, which has in all sorts of ways affected the position of women.

W.B. Apparently it was only the woman's consent that might be dispensed with. But do you suppose that these customs of expecting women to marry under orders were or are really enforced?

M.G. Of course, in matters of this kind law or

custom is often not decisive. At all times the woman can make her influence felt, whatever the law may be. Thus, even where child-betrothal is the custom, a girl may, when grown up, find a way of avoiding marriage. Among the Australian tribes, if a girl

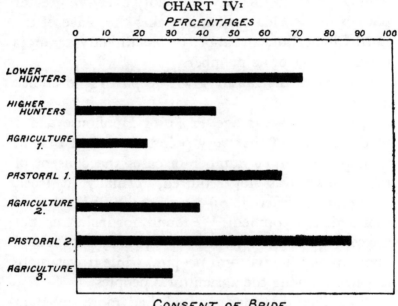

CHART IV[1]

CONSENT OF BRIDE
Ratio of Cases when it is not required to all Cases Recorded.

dislikes the man to whom she was betrothed as a child, she runs away with her lover. She is then pursued by her relations and her betrothed, and there may be a fight. She is brought back, but if she resists and runs away again, she is allowed her way, though

[1] The chart is based on figures given in *The Material Culture and Social Institutions of the Simpler Peoples*, by L. T. Hobhouse, G. C. Wheeler, and M. Ginsberg, p. 153.

her lover has to make formal expiation by allowing her relations to beat him or throw spears at him.

W.B. I should look out for a girl whose relations were short-sighted and likely to be bad shots with a spear.

M.G. Another example may be given from an African people, the Ibos of Nigeria. A girl is usually betrothed in infancy and a sum of money is paid by the prospective husband to her father. When she is six or eight years old, however, she is consulted, and if she does not like her suitor her father will wait until she makes her own choice. Then he repays the first suitor whom she has rejected from the money handed over by the one whom she accepts. Among many primitive peoples elopement is a recognized method of concluding a marriage.

W.B. In principle, however, the primitive peoples seem to agree with Dr. Johnson. And I have an impression that, outside Britain and America, families still have a great deal to say about the marriages of their members.

M.G. Certainly. Apart from parental control in laws relating to the marriages of minors, the influence of the family, here as elsewhere, goes much deeper than the law. Marriages are still to a great extent a family as well as a private concern.

W.B. After all, the family does represent a substantial fund of experience and knowledge of life. There was possibly more to be said for Dr. Johnson than young people would allow to-day.

But we are in danger of becoming like the newspapers and sticking at section J. You and I are expected to discuss not match-making only but everything that the family as a social group does for its members. It helps to educate them, it helps them to enjoy their leisure, it may control or influence their choice of occupation.

M.G. Yes. Just as for the sociologist it is important to know how people come by their partners, so it is important to know how they come by their occupations; how much chance or individual choice enters into that and how much of guidance by the family or other institutions.

W.B. That's the point of our questions in section E as to how the first job was got or the reasons for choosing occupations.

M.G. From the answers, presumably, you will find that the State through the Labour Exchanges has there invaded territory which once belonged to the Family.

W.B. Just as sixty years ago the State took over education from the Family.

M.G. The State certainly hasn't done *that*. In spite of all that the State and other interested parties have done to take over education, most psychologists would still regard the Family as the principal educator; it exerts an enormous influence over the minds of the young.

W.B. Isn't the State, with its infant schools and its nursery schools, continually working back earlier and earlier into the life of the individual?

M.G. Yes, but psychologists keep pushing back earlier and earlier the years in which character and temperament are thought to be moulded. It has even been said that, in essentials, the child's attitude to the world around him is decided during his first two years.

W.B. To me that would take a lot of proving. Can a child under two really have learned to distinguish between truth and lies, or between mine and thine?

M.G. You must have that out with the specialists in child psychology.

W.B. I'd like to do so some day.

M.G. But everyone will agree that it is within the family that the child acquires his likes and dislikes, his hates and loves. It is the Family that teaches him what goods to seek, what pleasures to enjoy, what careers to admire and emulate. It is within the Family that he learns the meaning of co-operation and self-control, of loyalty, sympathy, and altruism. A hint of the truth of this is given in our very language. Such words as "kind," "liberal," "generous" show us by their derivation what qualities are rooted in the family circle. Again, whether a child shall be subservient or independent depends so largely on the influence of the parents. If the parents pretend to be omniscient or deceive the children for false appearance of certainty, children will tend to be cynical and distrusting and intellectually dulled. If, on the other hand, the parents admit their own fallibility, the child's curiosity and open-mindedness will be encouraged.

W.B. Of course, I agree with that. My point against the child psychologists is that most of that comes after the child's third birthday—after the child has become human, as a very efficient and devoted mother of two small boys once put it to me. Personally, I'm more interested in the other end of childhood, when the child is beginning to be a real companion to the parents and beginning usually to think of being a companion to someone else. Do you know whether the Family is tending, as some people say, to break up sooner, or how the ages at which children leave their homes now compare with the ages of leaving in the last generation?

M.G. I don't know of any figures about that at all.

W.B. So that what we learn about that from the Family Form will be quite new? I've noticed that we are getting very full answers there.

M.G. Good! But the Family's influence on people's careers doesn't stop when they leave home. If you consider occupation alone, sociologists have always been much interested in the question of what I may call "occupational mobility," that is to say the extent to which people's occupations were determined by the social or economic standing of their parents. In ancient times the social classes were very rigid, so that a person's birth fixed his job and position for life. In modern times equality before the law has been gradually established and legal privileges have disappeared, yet we find John Stuart Mill say that in his time the different grades of workers were so clearly marked off from each other as to remind him of the hereditary distinctions that we find in societies based on caste.

W.B. John Stuart Mill lived many years ago and the social ladder must have got a good deal broader since then.

M.G. Yes, nowadays we hear a great deal of the social ladder, but how many people does it raise? Is it long enough to reach from the lowest level of the casual and unskilled to the heights of the professional and administrative world? Is the movement steep and difficult or smooth and graded? Do the people who climb up stay up? Or do the children fall back to their previous family level? These are all questions upon which there is much argument and very little knowledge.

W.B. There will be more knowledge after this enquiry; but surely you have done something yourself to add to our knowledge there?

M.G. On a very small scale. Nothing like what we may hope to get from these forms of yours.

W.B. Didn't you yourself send out a form and find that people were much interested in saying what their fathers' and grandfathers' occupations had been?

M.G. Yes. I sent out a questionnaire and got more than three thousand answers, on points rather like sections E to H of the Family Form.

W.B. Did you get any definite results on this

particular question of what you call occupational mobility?

M.G. Yes, I think so.[1] I arranged my returns into three classes. The first class included professional men, large-scale employers, and men of independent means or men working on their own account. The second class included employers on a smaller scale, small shopkeepers, salaried officials. The third class included wage-earners: skilled, semi-skilled, and unskilled.

W.B. What did you find of movement between these classes from one generation to the next?

M.G. It looks as if it had recently become easier for men to rise. I found 12 per cent. of the present generation in the first class had parents in the third class; that is to say, had risen substantially in economic grade. In the last generation the corresponding figure was only 6 per cent. To this extent it has recently become easier for men to rise.

W.B. So that occupational mobility has increased. Do you think that increase has now gone far enough?

M.G. No. It ought to be easier for men to rise—and fall—according to their abilities. The downward movement in my returns is very slight. The Family into which one is born still largely determines one's place in life. In the professions, at least, the family pull is still generally decisive. For the legal profession,

[1] The full results were published in the *Economic Journal* for December 1929.

for instance, I made an analysis some years ago of the entries to Lincoln's Inn in the period from 1886 to 1927.

W.B. What was the main result?

M.G. Throughout the period the parents of those entering were for the most part either professional men themselves or landowners or employers, and it was only in the last few years that a tiny proportion of the skilled artisan class crept in; in all probability even these few were aided by war grants and are therefore exceptional.

W.B. That's only the legal profession, which is highly conservative.

M.G. Another analysis that I made of the occupations of families of candidates for the higher branches of the Civil Service shows that none came from the ranks of the workers. Medicine again is still practically closed to the lower social classes.

W.B. Surely, the development of the scholarship system is changing all that?

M.G. Of course, the educational ladder is beginning to lift a few, but it is quite a small proportion. It is estimated that something like four or five in a thousand elementary school children reach a University, and about twelve out of every hundred elementary school children are assisted in various ways to take a step higher up the educational ladder. As against that, the proportion estimated by competent authorities as capable of benefiting from higher education is 50 to 75 per cent.

W.B. I should put the percentage of people in all ranks, up to Cabinet Ministers, who would be the better for a course at the School of Economics at much more than 75 per cent. But that does not mean that, even if I thought the country could afford the money, I should set out at once to organize higher education on that scale. It is impossible to expand Universities very rapidly without lowering the quality of the teaching. You and I and America know how difficult it is to find or train enough competent teachers, and then there's the difficulty at the other end. It is of no use to give University education to more people than you can hope to find jobs for after they've been through the course. Before we enlarge the Universities greatly we must convince employers much more generally that University education is worth having.

M.G. Well, it is clear that we have not yet gone very far in providing opportunities for all those capable of benefiting from them. The scales are still heavily weighted against the poor student. It has been said that about 75 per cent. of the annual entry to the Universities pass in without any scholarships.

W.B. Are you sure of that figure? My recollection of the last *Report of the University Grants Committee* is that something like 50 per cent. of all University students in Britain have scholarships or similar assistance.[1]

---

[1] The actual percentage of full-time University students receiving assistance is given as 45·2 for the whole of Britain and 40·6 for England alone, in *Report of University Grants Committee* for 1928–29, p. 7.

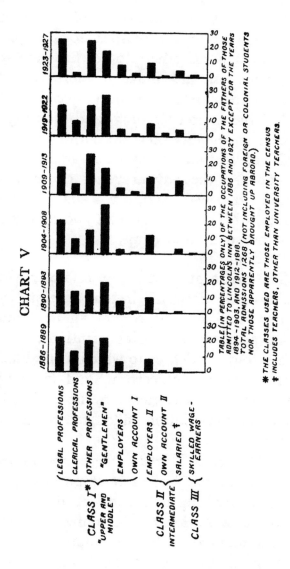

CHART V

M.G. The figure given to me may relate to some years ago, but that does not dispose of my argument. It is obviously easier for persons born in certain families than it is for others to get first-rate school teaching, which should make it more likely that they will get scholarships to the University: to say nothing of the better feeding and housing that they'll get from the day they are born.

W.B. Of course, that is so. But look here, Ginsberg, can you abolish the advantage of choosing one's father and mother well, and, if you could, ought you to try to do so? There are at least two serious arguments against such an attempt.

M.G. What are they?

W.B. The first argument is that a family which is successful is often successful, in part at least, because of inherited abilities: the son of an able man or woman is worth paying special attention to.

M.G. Yes, but the degree to which mental abilities are inherited is very uncertain, and training undoubtedly has a great deal to do with ability. Nurture, as Francis Galton called it, is as important as Nature.

W.B. But even if Nurture were not merely as important as Nature, but more important, so long as you allow anything to Nature at all, you ought to give special attention to the sons of people who have shown marked ability. Human beings begin with different natures and they don't get their natures by chance. To aim at mathematical equality of opportunity for every individual doesn't seem to me a good social policy.

M.G. Major Leonard Darwin, at least, would agree with *you*. He was recently President of the Eugenics Society, and said once that "Equality of opportunity would lead to a progressive lowering of the standard of civilization, a decline to which no assignable limit can be placed short of savagery and famine." *I* am inclined to prefer the authority of Francis Galton, who was the father of Eugenics, and who taught that: "The best form of civilization would be one in which education was not costly, where incomes were chiefly derived from professional sources and not much through inheritance, and where every lad had a chance of showing his abilities and, if highly gifted, was enabled to achieve a first-class education."

W.B. I don't disagree with a word of that, since I don't suppose that Francis Galton contemplated that all incomes from professional sources, by which he meant all earned incomes, whether called wages or salaries or fees, should be equal. So that the father who proved his special value by earning highly would be able to do more for his children than other fathers. That brings me to my second difficulty—about absolute equality of opportunity. Is it consistent with family life? Is not every family engaged in trying to do as well as possible for its young people—to do better than other families? If parents have no chance or hope of doing this, won't they lose one of their main incentives in life? Absolute mathematical equality of opportunity for each individual means, not merely that the State helps all and sundry, but that, by taxation or otherwise, it prevents the successful family from giving special help to its own members.

M.G. That comes to saying that to some extent the Family as a social group stands for inequality of opportunity as between individuals.

W.B. I think it does, because the Family is a succession of individuals and because the Family does not judge its own members, and never will judge its own members, with cold-hearted, impartial detachment.

M.G. How far would you carry this principle of inequality of opportunity through the Family and what does it mean in practice?

W.B. I'd rather say what it doesn't mean. First, it doesn't mean accepting and defending just as it stands the existing unequal distribution of wealth and of opportunities based on wealth. From the eugenic point of view, there's much to be said for thinking, as Galton suggested, that wealth goes too much by inheritance and too little for services. That's only from the eugenic point of view; I'm not speaking for the moment as an economist.

Second, it doesn't mean that the State shouldn't give scholarships or spend money in cheapening education. Just as each human family does the best it can for *its* bright boys and girls, so the State, as head of the larger family of all its citizens, should step in, to secure that high gifts, wherever they appear, win through to opportunity.

M.G. Hardly anyone will quarrel with those two negatives. Certainly I shan't. But what of your principle?

W.B. My principle also is really a negative. It points, not to something that the State should do, but to things that it should avoid. The State shouldn't treat human beings as if they came into the world apart from their families, and thus ignore heredity. And the State shouldn't destroy all possibility for each family to do the utmost for its members, to do better, if it can, for them than other families do for their members. My principle, however, isn't a class distinction. One may have good and bad parents in all classes. And in all classes one must leave something for the Family to do, to favour its own young people.

M.G. That is a side of the Family which has caused many people to attack it. In this respect the Family is like other social groups, which often begin for the purpose of mutual aid and service but develop a collective egoism towards the rest of the world. Some of the most villainous secret societies in America began as societies for mutual comfort and support. So did Tammany itself.

W.B. That's a danger with all voluntary associations—churches and religious orders and trade unions and many more. But it might not be easy to get on without churches and trade unions, for all that.

M.G. It is on this score that Plato attacked the private family and wished to replace it, for the ruling classes at least, by a communal life, in which family affection might extend to the whole group.

W.B. Of which Aristotle said that it would be a very watery affection.

M.G. And in our own time the Family has been attacked again on very similar grounds. Of our middle-class home life Mr. Bernard Shaw says that: "It is no more natural to us than a cage is to a cockatoo. Its great danger to the nation lies in its narrow views, its petty tyrannies, its false social pretences, its endless grudges and squabbles."

W.B. I suspect, Ginsberg, that the Family will survive Bernard Shaw as it has survived Plato.

M.G. So do I, Director.

W.B. Let's leave it there.

VI

SOME PROBLEMS FOR SOLUTION

A Discussion between Sir William Beveridge (*W.B.*) and Mrs. J. L. Adamson (*J.L.A.*)

W.B. I was wondering, Mrs. Adamson, as we came into the studio together, whether you noticed one argument against abolishing all distinctions between men and women.

J.L.A. I didn't notice anything in particular. What do you mean, Sir William?

W.B. My point is that we didn't really come in together. The door is too narrow. So you, without noticing anything in particular, went first, and I followed. If we'd both been merely equal men we might both have tried to go first and have stuck in the doorway, or we might have stayed outside, bowing and scraping and giving way to one another, and not been in our places here at the microphone when the red light began to flicker.

J.L.A. That would have been unfortunate. I'll let you walk out first at the end, if you like.

W.B. Thank you very much. I'm afraid I was going to ask for rather more than that. One or other of us to-night must have the last word. I was hoping that, on the principle of sex equality, you'd leave that to me.

J.L.A. Of course not. It's the traditional right of every woman to have the last word. That's well known to all *married* men, Sir William.

W.B. So that if at the end I behave like a married man and a gentleman and leave the last word to the lady, all will be well. But if I try to behave as your equal——

J.L.A. We may go on answering one another and fighting for the last word till the b.b.c. lose their temper and cut us off in the middle.

W.B. That would be as unfortunate as it would have been for us not to begin in time. These small sex conventions save a lot of trouble. There are many other time-saving customs—like letting the woman one is with have the first chance of a seat in trams, or the man finding the small change for cabs and tips and meals.

J.L.A. The young women to-day say that that last custom must have gone out with crinolines or at least in the war. Anyhow, those conventions don't matter. No woman cares a bit about them.

W.B. And no man minds them. That's why they are likely to continue. But when one comes to sex differences that really matter, that people do badly want to abolish in the name of sex equality, then trouble may begin. Take this emancipation of married women that Mr. Justice McCardie talks of. I'm all for it myself, in principle, and I've no doubt that it makes married life more interesting, but it must also make married life more complicated.

J.L.A. In what way more complicated? Many married women, I know, have welcomed what Mr. Justice McCardie has said.

W.B. Our fathers had a saying about marriage, that if two people ride on a horse, one of the two must ride behind. They called that a bit of common sense—*horse sense.* The man rode in front and held the reins; his wife sat behind firmly strapped to him. She could peer over his shoulder and try to guess where they were going, and whisper in his ear, and pinch him when she was cross. But with a good thick skin he didn't mind that, and he could kick her in return. All very simple and satisfactory—to our fathers. To-day marriage isn't like that. Marriage *à la* McCardie is more like two people riding abreast on the same horse, doing a rather difficult balancing feat and each holding one rein. It's more companionable than the old way, but it's more complicated, and must at times be rather confusing to the horse.[1] How do married couples decide which way they're going when they disagree now that each has an equal voice? Perhaps I ought to ask first, Mrs. Adamson, whether you think that there is a real difference from the good old days, whether wives now do have more to say than their mothers had?

J.L.A. I am sure that wives to-day have a great

---

[1] Dr. Johnson, when this simile was put to him by Mr. Dilly, expressed the view that with such riding the horse would throw both partners.

deal more say—more than their mothers used to have—on all kinds of matters, not only in the Family but on national and international affairs.

W.B. And their husbands don't mind? One of the people who has filled in our Form says that the chief trouble in family life is the intolerable way in which some husbands object to their wives not behaving like the husbands' mothers. And a very clever friend of mine once told me that what's wrong with the average man is that he marries a girl because she's the opposite of his mother and he then spends the rest of his life trying to make her just like his mother.

J.L.A. I'm sorry for him. Of course, some men are very conservative. But they do now recognise that women have gained citizenship and become entitled to public life. You'll get miners', engineers', and labourers' wives all talking politics hard, and often disagreeing with their husbands in politics.

W.B. They can disagree about things like politics without upsetting anybody. Where one puts a cross on a ballot paper doesn't matter much. But where one puts the sideboard or the gramophone matters a great deal.

J.L.A. No, no, Sir William, to my mind it is more important where one puts a cross on a ballot paper than the position of the sideboard or gramophone.

W.B. I'm sure that you're an exceptional woman, Mrs. Adamson. But what about more serious family problems—about the place of living, the use of leisure, and the place for holidays, the education of the children; how do husbands and wives settle those things now when they differ?

J.L.A. My experience is that things like education of children are left to the mother. Naturally she consults with father, but in the end it's she who has to decide whether she can make the sacrifice to send them to a higher school or the University, and it's she who finds the house and manages the family.

W.B. That sounds like saying that equality of the sexes means that women get their own way. But I wonder whether they really do. Of course, if the husband has agreed that the wife shall have the spending of practically the whole family income, it is she who decides how to spend it—on better education for the children or on a better house or on a good time in the holidays or on saving for old age. But suppose the husband definitely prefers one of these things to the others, or prefers some of his personal pleasures—isn't it he then that is going to decide over the head of his wife? Isn't the family income still mainly the husband's income, in law and in fact?

J.L.A. There's much more financial consultation between husband and wife than there used to be.

W.B. Do you mean that it is not so common—at any rate among working-class families—for the husband just to give a fixed sum, thirty shillings or two pounds, out of his wages to the wife and keep all the rest?

J.L.A. There is much less of that. It is much more common with good husbands for them just to keep their necessary expenses and hand over the rest to the wives. That happens partly because, instead of spending the evenings away from their families, in a club or public-house, more men spend the evening at the pictures *with* the family, or at home——

W.B. Or at home, listening to you and me. Let's say a good word for the B.B.C., if we fairly can. But on this point of financial consultation, I want to ask you something. As a good Socialist, Mrs. Adamson—I suppose, by the way, that you are a Socialist?

J.L.A. I'm a member of the Labour Party.

W.B. Like other members of that party, you must often have said in public speeches that political emancipation alone doesn't bring freedom; it must be followed by economic emancipation; economic pressure may be as effective as the law to make men slaves.

J.L.A. I've certainly said that, and it's true.

W.B. Probably it is. But so far as that is true in the State, isn't it true also in the Family? In spite of Mr. Justice McCardie, is a married woman really free, able to determine her own destiny, if she has to ask her husband for every penny she spends while she is with him, and if by years of wifehood and motherhood all other occupations have practically become closed to her, so that she can't leave him? Do we solve this problem of the economic dependence of married women by talking of financial consultation?

J.L.A. Certainly not. But what more would you propose?

W.B. Let me put to you what I call the Russian Theory. I suppose that, like the rest of us, you have read about Russia and what the Government is said to be doing there to equalize the position of the sexes and to give economic independence to women, when bearing children not less than at other times. All men and women, as I understand, have jobs, and marriage is a free contract, lasting only so long as both parties want it to last. If there are no children, each goes on working. If there are children, the mother gets a holiday on full pay for so many months before and after birth; a certain proportion of the father's wages is deducted, before he gets it, and is handed over to the mother, if she is looking after the child, or to the nursery, if she has put it into a public nursery and gone back to work; this deduction continues, whether the marriage continues or not. The mother needn't, of course, send the child to a nursery if she doesn't want to, but in many ways that is easier than looking after it herself, because house-room for most people is too limited to let them keep children in their homes. And the mother needn't go on living with the father, for the sake of the children, or for an income, a day longer than she wants to. That is complete equality of the sexes and economic emancipation of married women.

J.L.A. I've never been to Russia, and I don't know how things work out there.

W.B. Nor have I been to Russia, and I can't say how far that description is true of any large part of the population. But whether it's true to fact or not doesn't matter. It's just as interesting as a theory and an example of what might be involved in giving women, not legal independence only, but economic independence. Of course, it's not only equality of the sexes that the Russians are after. They seem also to be making a definite drive against the Family—just in the spirit of Plato 2,300 years ago—on the ground that family affection breaks men's loyalty to the State, and turns them into self-seekers, for their wives and children. I'd like to come back later to my doubts about the Russian Theory on that side. Meanwhile, what do you think of it as a means of giving real equality to men and to women?

J.L.A. It's very interesting. But I believe that British people will want to work out legal and economic independence for married women, possibly by some different method. The vast majority of married women in this country, though they have a growing interest in public affairs, prefer to be home-builders, rather than to seek paid employment outside the home.

W.B. But what *are* your different methods for giving economic freedom to women? Are family allowances, paid to the mother direct for the maintenance of the children, one of the methods?

J.L.A. I'm whole-heartedly in favour of family allowances, though I hadn't looked at them mainly in that light.

W.B. Or would you like to see a definite proportion of the husband's income legally secured to the wife, or part of his property made over to her, as compensation for giving up her earning career on marriage?

J.L.A. I'm not ready to say "yes" or "no" to definite questions like that. British people will work gradually to greater economic independence for women in marriage. But it's not yet as practical a question as many others. I'm constantly attending meetings of women where they are free to discuss anything they like; it's hardly ever that this question of economic dependence is brought up as a serious grievance. It's not yet a burning question.

W.B. I hope you're right, for I don't quite see the solution of this question, if it does become a burning one. And no doubt you are right about the working women. I think there has probably been more resentment of economic dependence among the wives of professional and business men and middle-class people generally than among the people you have in mind. And I can see reasons why there should be.

J.L.A. Yes, after all, the working women feel that they render useful service in the home and are performing work of the highest national importance.

W.B. Of course. But instead of pursuing that,

Mrs. Adamson, I'd like to go back, if I may, to something else that you said just now.

J.L.A. What was that?

W.B. About home-building. You said that most women in this country would prefer to be home-builders to being anything else. Many men now say that home-building by women is a lost art, or at least a decaying staple industry.

J.L.A. What do they mean, Sir William? Is that another way of saying that women ought not to take an interest in outside affairs—that they ought not to go into politics?

W.B. As you have done, Mrs. Adamson. No, I wasn't thinking of that. I wasn't thinking, either, of what Dr. Dalton and Mrs. Barton discussed, of how household work is being reduced by labour-saving devices and by buying outside the food and clothes that were once prepared at home.

J.L.A. Of course, there is more leisure in the home than there used to be.

W.B. But isn't the greater leisure due mainly to something more important than tinned food or gas-cookers? Isn't it that there are fewer young children to nurse and wash and dress and feed and scold? That's what men mean when they say that home-building is a decaying industry. Home means family, and women aren't building families, not as they used to, at least.

J.L.A. That's the crux of the matter. There's a revolt against large families. Not many women of my generation, if they were young again now, would set out to have as many children as they had.

W.B. Why wouldn't they? Are they affected by economic considerations? Would they have more children if they had family allowances? A good many people have urged that view upon me.

J.L.A. I don't believe that family allowances would have much effect on the birth-rate. A great many working women feel that bearing children is too dangerous—they don't get a square deal and the same attention as richer women. Three thousand of them pass out every year, and many thousands more lose their health.

W.B. No doubt that number ought to be reduced, but three thousand is a small proportion in more than six hundred thousand births each year. It can't be merely or mainly the fear of dying in childbirth that stops the children coming.

J.L.A. No, the women simply do not feel entitled to bring children into the world unless they can give the children a chance of a decent life, unless they are sure that there's room for them.

W.B. There will be plenty of room, if each family has only one or two children, because there will be many families without any children and there will be people who do not marry. You may get the population disappearing.

J.L.A. Won't that right itself automatically? If there comes to be more room for people, perhaps more will be born?

W.B. Why should they? The fall of the birth-rate didn't come when people were beginning to be poorer or to feel poorer; it came just when the opening out of the New World was making everybody richer, with more room. Before the fall began, the size of the population was determined, one may say, automatically; it was the net result of the working of the sex instinct, leading to births, and of illness and old age, leading to death. But if the sex instinct is not going to lead to births, maintenance of population will depend upon finding enough couples who want children, a husband and wife who have paternal and maternal instincts, and not sex instinct only.

It will be like another problem of which we hear so much to-day—that of currency, in which also we have to pass from an automatic to a managed system. In each case there's the difficulty that the management rests upon the private decisions of individuals, without any certainty that what the individuals think best for themselves will add up into what is best for the community. I am not saying that what is now happening to the birth-rate is bad, but I do think that in fifty years' time the civilised States of the world may all be up against the problem of maintaining populations. Presumably the States will want to go on existing.

J.L.A. Is there any doubt that they'll be able to do so?

W.B. On the whole I think they will be able.

SOME PROBLEMS FOR SOLUTION

Probably there are paternal and maternal instincts in a sufficient number of people to keep up the population.

J.L.A. I'm certain that there is a real desire for children in most women.

W.B. And probably in most men. But the question is: Are we going to get enough people wanting enough children and making their desire effective? You need to have both husband and wife wanting children now, and not one or two children only.

J.L.A. Aren't enough children being born now to keep up the population?

W.B. At the moment in Britain, I believe, *not* enough. The calculation isn't a perfectly simple one, but I saw that Professor Carr-Saunders a few days ago, in commenting on the latest birth-rate figures, said that we were not replacing ourselves now.[1] If the present birth-rate continued long enough, he said, our population would die out.

J.L.A. Did Professor Carr-Saunders propose any remedy?

W.B. He himself wasn't pessimistic. He thought that, when it became necessary, an appeal to the most responsible part of the population to keep up our numbers would certainly succeed. They would become the parents of the future. The less responsible, not caring about the needs of the community and preferring freedom to the burden of children, would tend to eliminate themselves.

[1] In the *Observer*, March 13th, 1932.

J.L.A. Do you agree with that?

W.B. Not altogether. I should like to see it happen, but I'm not sure that it will happen. To begin with, we've no reason for believing that the birth-rate will stay even as high as it is. So many people may prefer freedom to children, that the contribution of children to the community that has to be demanded of the responsible people (as Professor Carr-Saunders calls them) may be too high for them. Next, I'm not sure what motives will move the "responsible" people. I'm not sure that anybody will care much about producing children for the community.

Here, if you'll allow me to make rather a long speech, I'll come back to what I've called the Russian Theory—that in the interests of sex equality, infant welfare, and communal feeling one should, in effect, break up the Family. If, according to the Russian model, there is going to be nothing but a cash *nexus* between father and son, if we say to people: Once the child is born it will be taken off your hands, subject to a financial adjustment, and you can go on living your own life, you needn't worry about the family. I want answers to a lot of questions: First, is anybody going to have children at all? Second, is anybody, except a few people to whom their work is an absorbing vocation, going to have a sufficient motive for trying to get on in life? Third, is life going to be interesting and old age even remotely tolerable? Everybody knows how fathers and mothers slave and scrape, and incidentally add to the wealth of the world, in the effort to give their children a better chance in life. If that objective goes, if the economic motive is going to be limited to trying to get more food or better clothes or housing for oneself, what a sordid business life will be. And how dull! Most people's jobs are pretty dull and nearly all hobbies wear thin in time. I don't see us safely dispensing with the Family as an economic motive and an interest in life for the common man. We mustn't tell him not to worry about the Family. It's worrying about the Family that keeps grandfather young.

J.L.A. And grandmother, also. Don't forget her.

W.B. And granny, too. But while I see those objections to the Russian Theory, I've also some unanswered questions about our own system. *Question 1:* May not the children be looked after better by experts collectively than individually by untrained mothers, carrying on by tradition? *Question 2:* Is the Family in the last resort consistent with the economic independence of wives and mothers? *Question 3:* Is the Family as it stands and as it is developing going to give us enough population and the right sort of population? Of course I don't expect *you* to answer those questions. They're the problems for consideration and solution by all of us.

J.L.A. I wish the Government would pay more attention to them. We all talk about children being the greatest asset of the nation, but we do very little to show that we believe it.

W.B. I can see why Governments shouldn't do much. Governments are taken up with immediate problems—with to-day or, at most, with to-morrow. The problems I've named, or at least the last two, aren't immediate; they're for the day after to-morrow. I'm content to take it from you that economic dependence on their husbands in marriage isn't yet felt by most women as a serious grievance, though if the drive for sex equality continues it may in time become so. And for the moment, also, we seem to have enough people in the country. Because these questions are not yet burning, there's the more chance of thinking them over quietly beforehand, and there's every reason for all of us to do so—to be ready to deal with them, not in a flurry, but calmly and wisely, when they do arise. That's what we've been after with these talks about the Family and with this investigation, both to get people thinking about vital problems and by the help of those who fill in the form to collect the facts for sound judgment.

That's been our object, Mrs. Adamson; I don't know how much you and they feel that it has been accomplished.

J.L.A. What *I* feel, Sir William, is that you've had a great time propounding views on what you are pleased to term the "Russian Theory," the economic dependence of women, and also on the population question.

You're an economist, and economists, I'm told,

SOME PROBLEMS FOR SOLUTION

are particularly fond of putting up all sorts of controversial questions which neither they nor anyone else can answer. I suppose you do it to stimulate discussion, and I'm sure that these problems should engage the attention of all thoughtful men and women.

W.B. There's certainly plenty to discuss. Even in six talks we couldn't deal with all sides of the Family.

J.L.A. In fact you and I haven't even touched on the relations of parents and children.

W.B. Perhaps that's as well. You and I could hardly have discussed that properly by ourselves. We'd have needed one of the young people here to help us; the young people have views, you know. But on what we have discussed, you've been so kind in answering my questions as well as letting me make long speeches, that I was wondering if after all——

J.L.A. What?

W.B. You wouldn't relent and let me have that last word.

J.L.A. No, Sir William, you've had such a good innings that I feel I must stick to the woman's traditional right to have the last word. I want to say that I hope every mother who hears of it will help you in this scheme of investigation and will send for the Family Form, see that it is well filled up and returned to the B.B.C.

After all, the Family is mother's business and her greatest interest.

More especially would I appeal to working-class women to help, so that our conditions will not be left out of the picture which you, Sir William, will paint after all the Family Forms have come in.

So here's good luck to the scheme.

VII

THE ENDURING FAMILY: A FIRST IMPRESSION OF THE RETURNS

In this chapter are given some first impressions of the Family returns received up to the beginning of April 1932. They are first impressions only, not definite results. It will be impossible to say what definite results may emerge from the returns till their statistical analysis has been completed—a task of many months. This chapter aims only at giving some impression of the kind of information that has come in and the kind of people from whom it has come. It is based on a hasty survey of as many forms as possible, and a careful reading and sampling of a few hundreds.

The first and much the strongest impression that one gets in reading these returns is of the interest and care with which they have been made. The form is not a short and easy one; filling it up is not an affair of a few minutes. It has twelve sections lettered from A to M—each with any number of questions. To fill the whole form fully may take a person used to such work an hour and a half or two hours; it must have taken many of those who sent in returns much more than that.

I thought myself that most people, even if they wanted to fill in something, would be content to answer only those sections which in the instructions are named as most essential: the Reference section A, section B, which gives marriage dates and ages, and section D, which gives the actual children of the marriage.

I was quite wrong in this expectation: most of those who sent the form back have filled substantially the whole of it. 90 per cent. and upwards have answered not only the sections A, B, and D, but also E—occupations and earnings of husband, wife, and children; G—husband's and wife's parents and their marriage and occupations; H—husband's and wife's brothers and sisters; and J—place of meeting of partners.

The only section of general application which was not answered by more than 90 per cent. was F—on Family Expenditure, and there we got answers from over 60 per cent. Finally, there was M—the most difficult section of all, on "Changes and Forces in Family Life," which I put at the end, so as not to frighten people, but we have answers in that section from 70 per cent. There is one section (C) as to previous marriage, which applies, of course, only to a very few people; there is another (K) for remarks, and there is another (L) for offering further information. These naturally were not filled in by most people, though as many as one in four have offered further information in section L.

The result of this fullness with which the forms have been filled is that each separate form contains a great deal of information. It deals as a rule, not with one husband and wife and their children, but with parents, grand-parents, brothers and sisters, children's marriages and children's children. On most forms we find three complete families—a husband and wife in section B and their children, the family in which the husband was born, and the family in which the wife was born. Taking a sample of 500 forms we found that, on an average, each recorded just under six marriages and nearly twenty-eight separate persons. Seven thousand forms—and we have already close on that number—will give us something like 18,000 families, 40,000 marriages, 180,000 separate persons—after allowing for uncertainties and duplications. The marriages stretch over every decade in the nineteenth century, and there are a substantial number for every decade from 1850 to 1930. There is any amount of work for statisticians in that.

The care and interest with which forms have been filled is the first impression; the fullness with which all sections have been answered is the first surprise. From what parts of the country and from what sort of people have these forms come?

A preliminary answer to the first part of this question is given graphically in the chart on p. 124. This shows the distribution of the Family returns among fifteen principal districts of Britain, and compares this distribution with that of population and of wireless licences. That is to say, it shows of 100 of

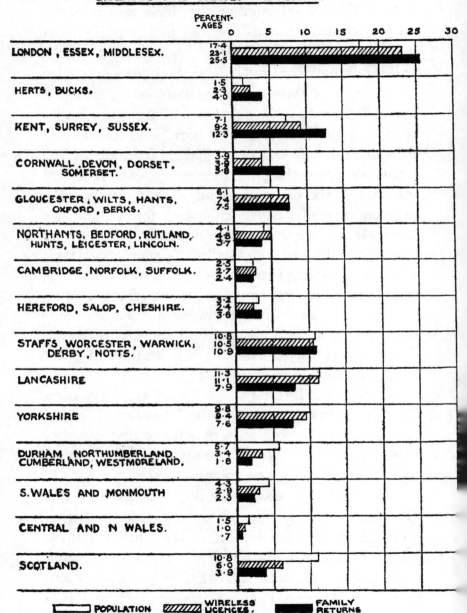

THE ENDURING FAMILY

population, of 100 wireless licences, and of 100 Family returns respectively how many are found in each district.[1]

Where the shaded rectangle (representing wireless licences) is longer than the white one (representing population) as in London, Essex, and Middlesex, this means that in that district there is more than the average number of licences per head of population; where the shaded rectangle is shorter than the white one, as in Scotland, this means that there is less than the average number of licences per head of population. Similarly, comparison of the black rectangle (representing Family returns) with the other two shows whether in any particular district there is in proportion to population and to wireless licences more or less than the average number of Family returns.

Comparing, first, population and wireless licences, we see that broadly over the whole south of England there is more than the average number of wireless licences per head of population in Britain; while in Scotland, Wales, and the extreme north of England wireless licences are below the average; in between, in the Midlands, Lancashire, and Yorkshire, they are about the average. Looking, next, at the Family returns, we see that these have come in more than in proportion either to population or to licences from

[1] For the Family returns the chart combines the results of two samples of 500 each (Numbers 300 to 800 and 3,600 to 4,100). The results of the two samples do not differ seriously.

the south and west of England, rather less from Lancashire and Yorkshire, and still less from the extreme north of England and Scotland. In the east of England and the Midlands they have come pretty well in proportion to population and licences. In England, the mining areas and those occupied by depressed staple industries have, as might be expected, sent fewer Family returns proportionately than other districts. In Scotland the position is obscured by taking the country as a whole, though this is necessary since the census figures for the separate counties in 1931 have not yet been issued. Actually from the industrial centre of Scotland—Edinburgh, Lanark, Renfrew, Dumbarton, Linlithgow, Stirling, Fife—Family returns have come in more than in proportion to licences, though less than in proportion to population, the number of licences per head being very low in that district. On the other hand, in the north of Scotland there are proportionately more licences but fewer Family returns.

While, however, these differences are interesting, the main result of the comparison in the chart is to show that on the whole the Family returns have come in substantial proportions from all parts of the country. This is more important than minor variations from one district to another.

The forms are spread fairly evenly by districts. How are they spread by economic grade? In section A of the form those filling it have been asked to classify the husband's occupation as being that of wage-earner, salaried person, employer, or worker on own account. Of every hundred forms about twenty come from families where the husband is a wage-earner, fifty-five from families where he is salaried, ten from employers, and fifteen from people working on their own account. These figures show that, as compared with others, wage-earners are at present much under-represented in the returns; instead of being about one-fifth of the whole they ought to be three-quarters.

That does not mean that there are not plenty of people of limited means in the form; of those who are salaried, a few have a total family income under £150 a year, more than one-quarter are under £300 a year, and more than half are under £500 a year. Of the wage-earners about 45 per cent. are under £150 of total family income, and another 45 per cent. are between £150 and £300; 7 per cent. are between £300 and £500, and 3 per cent. of the wage-earner families have more than £500 a year.

Just as wage-earners as such are under-represented, so naturally the poorest families in the country are under-represented; so, apparently, are the richest. The great bulk of the forms—nearly two-thirds—come from people with between £300 and £800 a year; that is, of total family income, not husband's earnings only. It is to people of the middle economic grades that this enquiry has appealed most strongly. For that, I think, there is a definite reason, which I will come back to later. For the moment I want to make it clear that the fact that wage-earners and the poorest families generally are not represented in their due proportions in our returns does not in the least destroy the value of the returns. It lessens the value of what one can say about the classes which are under-represented, but doesn't prevent one from reaching some conclusions even about them. And it hardly affects the value of the returns for other economic classes at all. How great that value is going to be, what is going to come out of the forms, there is no means yet of guessing. We may find—one always does find—all sorts of unsuspected pitfalls, as our statistical analysis gets to work. We can only say that the care and accuracy with which the returns seem to have been made is very encouraging, and there are plenty of them. The idea with which some critics of our enquiry started, that, since there are eight or nine million families in Britain, one cannot learn anything about changes of Family life without examining all the families or a large proportion, is too fantastic to need refutation.

But to say positively what we can hope to learn we must wait until we have done our statistical analysis. The most interesting and important results do not appear in a first impression. Of course, one or two things that statistics will bring out are beginning to show in a cursory inspection.

One sees decline of birth-rate at work, in innumerable individual cases—where a husband with thirteen brothers and sisters and wife with six have two children only, or a husband with three brothers and wife with five also have two children only; one professional man gives numbers in three generations; in each of the four families of his own and his wife's grandparents were on an average 8½ children; in the two families in which he and his wife were born there were on an average 5½ children; in his own there are only two.

One sees again that we are going to learn very interesting things about change or persistence of occupations from one generation to another. In the handful of forms which I have looked at carefully I have come across striking cases where the families of both husband and wife have had one and the same occupation for three generations back: on one form they were all bank managers or bank officials; on another all farmers. One comes across other striking cases of rapid change of economic grade. Whether fixity, or what Professor Ginsberg in his discussion with me called economic mobility, is going to predominate, we cannot tell till we have been through all the forms. Anyhow, it is clear that people have been much interested in giving their parents' and grandparents' and relations' occupations.

They've equally been much interested in thinking back on how they and others of their family came to meet their respective partners. This section J has been filled in in 95 per cent. of the cases, and often for more than one generation. But though naturally one always glances at section J, there is no doubt which are the two points that on a first survey are most interesting. One is the reason given (in section E) for choice of occupation; the other is section M —on Changes and Forces in Family Life.

In regard to choice of occupations, I was specially interested to compare the position of men and of women. To do this, I grouped the reasons given under three main heads: Parents' Choice or Influence, Own Choice or Aptitude, and "Necessity" (with which I put answers like "Chance" or "No choice"). There were, of course, references to other influences, such as advice of a schoolmaster, or winning a prize for music, but most of these clearly amounted to "own choice" or "aptitude." Just a little unexpectedly to me, in the forms I looked at, the scope of "own choice" turned out to be as great for women as for men. The parents' influence applied more often to the sons than to the daughters, fathers putting their sons into a family business or hereditary trade or counselling safety (this came several times) in the Civil Service or banking. So there were proportionately more men than women in my first group of "Parents' Choice." On the other hand, there were more women than men in my third group, of "Necessity"; there were more women than men who felt that they had had no choice at all, had become governesses or gone into domestic service or something else they did not care for, because there was nothing else to do. The reason for choosing domestic service was given by one woman as "Hated it:

wanted to be a teacher"; there were others also who became teachers unwillingly. So do some men become bank officials through their fathers' desire for safety, others "through lack of imagination or help." With proportionately more men in the first group (of parents' choice) and more women in the third group (of necessity or no choice) the middle group of own choice or aptitude bulks about equally for the two sexes. Clergyman, printer's operative, sawyer, tea-salesman, physician, naval officer, master-mariner ("for adventure"), science master, railway porter, petroleum technologist, journalist, librarian—these are all occupations given as chosen by the men themselves. Choices by women have a narrower range and are generally teacher, dressmaker (though one at least regrets this), nurse, or masseuse. There is a pleasant touch about a husband and wife who both give their occupations (Civil Servant and teacher) as chosen by their parents, but, while not regretting this, hope that their sons and daughters will be able to choose for themselves.

I now come to the last section of all, which to me has been the greatest surprise. That is section M, in which each person was asked to state "the chief changes as between your parents' generation, your own generation, and the generation after yours" in the relations of husband and wife, relations of parents and children, and family life generally. This was much the most difficult part of the form, and I did not expect many people to fill it; in fact, it has been filled in 70 per cent. of the cases, and, what is more interesting still, it has been filled for the most part by obviously normal people with happy family lives. When the form was first published one or two critics said that hardly anyone would fill it in except cranks and practical jokers. This criticism has fortunately proved quite unfounded. The cranks and practical jokers have hardly shown their heads.

Actually, what we have in section M is a symposium of views about family life and its changes and its problems by a class of people who are very seldom articulate, by ordinary people talking about the family life they know, not for effect, because their names are not going to be published, but because they find family life interesting as well as happy. One gets hardly any accounts of unhappy families, except here and again from a widow or widower.

Of course, section M is not going to be of much use to statisticians, but to sociologists it is fascinating. I cannot profess here to give more than a few hasty impressions. The first impression is that there have not been any very great changes in family life in the last generation, but what changes there are, are on the whole an improvement.

A tuberculosis officer, speaking less of himself than from his life experience of working-class families, sums it up by saying that "there is much less change in family life than newspapers would lead one to expect." He makes one other point on which I shall look forward to seeing the experience of others—

that is, that while girls tend to work outside and leave home more than they used, boys, in the more unsettled economic conditions of to-day, leave home less readily and seem to have become less adventurous than once they were.

"No revolutionary change" is undoubtedly the main theme of section M. There are some changes, but the real changes are less than the apparent or formal changes. There has been a loosening of family ties and authority and a strengthening of real ties; as a Civil Servant puts it, "a lot of sham family loyalty has been lost, but I do not find any lack of readiness to co-operate in a happy family life." Of course, the changed formal position of the wife and the resultant better companionship of husband and wife come out again and again in every class. "Woman has forged ahead so much in sport, industry, social and political life that no man, young or old, need hesitate at saying a woman is his friend and pal"—that is from an acetylene welder. "My wife," says another Civil Servant, "is freer to spend than her or my mother, but is no less economical on that account." "Our mothers were not allowed to handle any money or even know the amount of their husbands' income; now we often know more about it than our husbands," so speaks a farmer's wife. Her own chief difficulty in married life is that the duties of the farm make it impossible for her and her husband to go out together and so share pleasures, and as she so nicely thanks the wireless for helping her to overcome this, and even describes the filling in of the form as a shared pleasure, I feel I should like to make her a special acknowledgment. Another pleasant side of the new companionship of husband and wife is named by a Wesleyan minister as being greater readiness of husbands to take a share of housework.

Readers may remember how I asked Mrs. Adamson about the economic dependence of married women and whether this was resented. Her reply was that among the women she knew best it was not yet a burning practical question. Certainly, nearly all the forms I have read, whether coming from husbands or wives, confirm what Mrs. Adamson said; economic dependence of the wife in marriage to-day is hardly ever mentioned as a grievance or a difficulty. As one wife says, "Though the family income comes wholly from the husband, the wife is in partnership rather than a dependant."

Several people, indeed, suggest that the strengthening of real family ties which appears from so many forms is limited to the family in the narrower sense and is due to the parents and children becoming more nearly equal to one another and thus being better companions. Apart from parents and children, the ties seem to many people looser. Thus, a Sheffield workman says that, in his experience, brothers and sisters matter less to one another than they used to do, each choosing his or her own friends outside; this is confirmed by others. There also appears to be definitely less clannishness. "In my parents' generation," says one husband, "the affairs of brothers, sisters, uncles, aunts, and cousins were considered of very great interest and the family kept together, frequently visiting each other. I, and many of my friends, take little or no interest in our relations except our parents. It used to be customary for all the family to know the private affairs of all the others. This would now be resented." I am looking forward to seeing what others have to say on that.

Several people again dwell on the better choice of marriage partners that results from greater modern freedom of young people to meet one another and get to know one another's tastes and characters before they decide to marry. Certainly there was room for improvement here, as regards some sections of English society. I am not sure, indeed, that the difficulty of young people meeting, except in company with others, in the last generation, applied to more than a small section—of professional and wealthier people. With working people, I suspect, that there was always much more freedom. Here again, to look at more forms is going to be most interesting.

I could go on for ever quoting points of view and problems raised, even from this handful of forms that I have looked at carefully myself. I have no time to say even a word about the many interesting statements made about married women's employment—its reasons and its consequences. The forms are so interesting that, having read them once to get a few impressions for this chapter, I have read them all over again for interest. They give one what, so far as I know, no one has had in this country before—a composite picture of many happy families; of the families which have problems and struggles, but do not get into divorce courts or bankruptcy courts or police courts, or become the subjects of charity or official investigation. Their records are novels in real life: novels because their absolute anonymity makes one feel that one could never meet them, but real because they are real.

And there are already seven thousand of them. Let me say a few words about the number of returns.

I have no idea myself what proportion of returns one ought to expect in such a case as this, and I do not believe anyone else has. Most people, I think, who got 10 per cent. of replies to a circular would regard it as a great success; how many circulars get a response of even 3 per cent.? Actually we have already something like 13 per cent., and they are still pouring in. On the other hand, the form was not a circular sent out to everybody; it was sent, for the most part, only to people who asked for it, so that one might expect a larger response than to an ordinary circular. But then, again, this form was in other ways different from a circular asking for reply. It was an accompaniment of the talks; we advised everybody who was going to listen to send for the form, as making the talks more interesting, whether

THE ENDURING FAMILY

they filled in the form or not. And filling the form—at least the whole form—was a very stiff proposition.

If one sends out a single simple question—if one asks people in America whether they are for or against prohibition, or people in this country whether they are for or against a fixed Easter—one can count on answers by the hundred thousand, not by the thousand. But this long Family Form of twelve sections is not like that at all. When I first discussed numbers with the B.B.C. last December, I thought of printing 5,000 forms as a start, and getting back perhaps 1,000. I printed more only because the B.B.C. felt certain of disposing of more through societies co-operating with them. When the newspapers gave us so much publicity in February, I thought that if we issued 50,000 forms, as in fact we have done, we might get back 10,000, though I did not expect to have anything like so many facts upon them as we already have on 7,000 forms. Actually we may still get 10,000, for forms are still pouring in by the hundred.[1] I know from correspondence that many people have the forms and mean to send them in. I know that others are still sending for more forms. I hope that no one who is interested will be deceived by anything he reads or is told into thinking that the enquiry is at an end. There is really no fixed time-limit for receipt of forms, and though we have an abundance of facts already,

[1] The number by the end of April was 8,000, with forms still coming in.

more facts cannot hurt, and might help greatly, particularly for any districts or sections of the community not yet fully represented. We wanted plenty of forms to work on by the end of March, and we have plenty, but we can mix in others as they come, as they are still coming, by the hundred every day.

But whatever happens about that, we have already a most satisfying mass of facts to work on. We ought to be able to make an interesting and valuable social study out of that—just how interesting or valuable we cannot even begin to say till our work is nearly finished. No one can ever tell in advance what—whether anything—will be learned by any particular experiment in any field of science. But that is no reason for not experimenting. I wonder if the critics of the scheme have ever thought of that? If the response of listeners had proved disappointing, the experiment of these talks and this enquiry would still have been fully justified. The ways of getting the essential facts for social science are so limited that no way which offers any chance ought to be neglected.

In fact the response has been admirable in quality and very good in quantity. The Family Form was issued as part of a scheme of educational talks—of talks on the changing family as part of this changing world. Our first object—of stimulating thought about the varied problems of the Family—has clearly been achieved; that 50,000 forms should have been asked for is sufficient proof of that. Our second object—of securing response and help from listeners in getting new facts for advancing our knowledge of human society—has also been achieved on a large scale, though of course not on the same scale. Our scheme has appealed to people of every age and every economic grade. It has appealed most strongly—I give this as the last of my first impressions here—to people of the middle position, people of small means above the smallest. For that, I imagine, there are two reasons. One is that the wireless itself means more to such families than to others; they can afford the wireless, and they cannot afford so many other amusements as people who are better off, so many evenings away from home. The other reason is that it is in that middle economic grade that family problems are most interesting. I do not mean that parents in that grade are fonder of their children than others are. Of course they are not. But the poorer people have not the opportunity to do as much for their children or for so long. "In the working class," says one of them whom I have already quoted, himself in the lowest income grade of all, "it is very rare that parents take any interest in choosing occupations for their children; the main factor is money and as quickly as possible, more so where it is the eldest son of a large family about to commence his industrial life." I hope other workpeople will correct that for me if they think it is overstated. On the other hand, the richer people do not have so many material difficulties to overcome in educating children or placing them in careers or making the most of family income. "I do not think that poverty, unless extreme, is a cause of trouble," says a Civil Servant, at about £400 a year; "scheming together to make ends meet often draws husband and wife together." He is just in that middle class where contriving for the family is hard enough, but not too hard, a puzzle that just can be solved and that is the most interesting problem in the lives of most people.

APPENDIX

THE FAMILY FORM

This Appendix gives a list of the questions in the Family Form, with the Introduction and instructions for filling it up and returning it which were printed on the form. The questions are not set out with spaces for reply, as in the form itself. Copies of the form can still be obtained free of charge from the Publication Department of the B.B.C., Broadcasting House, Portland Place, W.1.

INTRODUCTION

To most men, for most of their lives, family relationships matter more than anything else, and are the most interesting things that happen. Nearly every human being born into the world is born into a family, has ancestors, parents, brothers and sisters, kindred. Nearly every human being, growing up in these relationships of family, or in later life, forming new relationships—to wife or husband, to children and their mates, perhaps to grandchildren—finds them a dominant influence in his fortunes and absorbing occupation of his thoughts. The respective advantages of early or later marriage, or of large or small families, the division and management of family income and the problem of married women's work, the launching of young people in careers and their matings, the change of occupations from one generation to the next, the keeping of children at home or the sending of them out to study, the changing relationships of young and old, husband and wife, brothers and sisters—all these things and others like them are matters about which nearly everyone at some time or other is forced to think.

But family relationships are not only the most interesting or most important things in life to most individuals. They are also among the most important and interesting subjects of scientific study.

The institution of the Family, though, in one form or another, it is found throughout the world and at nearly all stages of human history, is not at all the same thing everywhere or at all times. Like all our institutions it changes continually itself and it stands in changing relationship to other institutions, such as the tribe and the State. The Family has a history which it is absorbing to study and a future which it is fascinating to try to forecast. Looking back into the mists of antiquity or studying primitive races to-day, we may seek to trace the course along which the Family has travelled to reach the stage we know in Europe or America to-day. Estimating movements and forces from yesterday to to-day, we may try to guess where the Family will stand in this or some other country in the next generation, or in ten or a hundred generations. Astronomers, from the short observed movement of a comet during weeks or months, are able to lay down its track for centuries before and after. We shall never be able to do just that for the Family, but we can and ought to know more about it than we do. The laws that guide the development of human societies are more complex than are the laws of physics; they are also harder to discover, and to this day have been less studied; social science is in its infancy. That disadvantage, at least, we can do something to remove.

Making the Science of Society

Though in our understanding of social forces we may never attain the full light and certainty of the physical sciences, we need not live for ever in darkness. We can set out, in the patient spirit of those sciences, to gather facts about human nature and human society, to generalize from those facts and to test our generalizations by more facts.

In such an expedition, listeners are now invited to join, by filling in as accurately and as fully as possible this form of Family Return. There are some things which can be learnt about the Family from the census or from official records of births, deaths, and marriages. There are many more things essential to know which can be learned only if a sufficient number of families will make individual returns on such a form as this.

The form concerns all people in Britain who are married or have been married; it is an invitation to them to write down some facts about themselves and their families, and thereby to help in making science. Whether they are old or young, newly married or approaching their golden wedding, whether they have had children or not, whether their children are now living or dead, at home or away, very young or growing up or already grown up with homes of their own, all can help if they will. They can help by giving information which it is easy for them to give, which no one else can give, and which is vital to an understanding of perhaps the most important of all human institutions. And they can give this information anonymously, with all the secrecy of the ballot.

But though the form may be addressed primarily to married people, it is not addressed to them alone. Everybody is a member of a family, and those who are not married can help by giving facts about themselves, their parents, and the families in which they were born.

The form itself is necessarily a long one. The Family touches every man's life at every angle. The Family is not only a biological group, but an economic and a social group; it serves its members in many ways; its various aspects call for many separate sections in the form. There is, however, no need for anyone to fill in the whole form; still less is there need to fill it all in at once. Accurate information in almost any section will be worth sending in even by those who cannot or do not care to answer all the questions. But the fuller each answer the greater the service to science. Those who begin by trying to answer one part will, it is hoped, find it easy to go on. The successive weekly talks, discussing the various sides of family life, and explaining different sections of the form, will help in this.

When the forms have been received and tabulated, a summary of all the most interesting results will be given in further talks and published in a form accessible to listeners. How interesting those results will be depends on the extent to which listeners co-operate by filling in the form.

The form itself is an experiment. The questions will not fit all cases, and some of them may be puzzling to one person or another. But there is no question in the form that is asked for idle curiosity, that is not designed to throw light on some scientific issue now in doubt or further the solution of some problem of importance for human welfare. Though we are seeking light, however, on practical problems, the enquiry itself is purely scientific. Neither the talks nor the questions are directed to advocate or to secure material in support of any particular measure of reform or change. The object of the talks is to spread some of the knowledge that we have. The object of the form is to increase knowledge, under two main heads.

The first head has been named already. The Family as an institution has always been changing. In the last fifty years some aspects of it have changed with notable speed in the mechanical and economic transformation that has come over the civilized world. The first object of the form is to secure comparisons between successive generations of the same family group. To see how ages at marriage, numbers and spacing of children, occupations, economic and social relationships of the members of the Family, educational facilities and so forth have changed from one generation to the next is the way to get some idea of the future track of social development.

Nature and Nurture

The second head is as important. Every human being is moulded by two sets of forces, the nature which he inherits and the nurture which is imposed upon it. He is the product of his heredity and his environment. What nature contributes can be changed by man only with difficulty and very slowly, when it can be changed at all. What nurture contributes can be changed rapidly, by society if not by the individual. How much or how little, therefore, men of different natures differ from one another in bodily or mental faculties, how much of the differences that appear among men is due to nurture that is within social control, is thus an issue of prime importance.

It is an issue on which there have been many rash generalizations. It is approached here in the spirit of enquiry, without prejudging the issue.

In the facts of family life, heredity and a powerful environment are presented together for disentangling. In the Family appears both what is common to man and most animals—in mating and birth—and what most distinguishes him from them—as a reasoning, contriving, pre-eminently social creature. To study the Family is thus one of the most direct approaches to the knowledge of man's complex nature, to the ultimate goal of all social science. Every person who gets this form can help in that study by filling in the form, as week by week he listens to the talks about it.

THE FAMILY FORM AND HOW TO FILL IT

1. This form can be filled up by a married pair (the "Husband and Wife" of section B), or either of them, or by the survivor of such a pair, or by unmarried people for the families in which they were born.

2. The information supplied on this form for each individual and family is *secret* and will not be identified in any way with the persons to whom it relates.

3. There is *no need to fill up every section* of the form. If you can fill up only sections A, B, and D (and C if it applies), the information will be of value. Some people, by possessing family records or otherwise, will be able to answer more fully than others. But the more sections you can and do fill in correctly the better.

4. Where a *date* is asked for by day, month, and year, try to give it exactly. But if you cannot, give the month if possible as well as the year. If you do not know even the month, give the year only.

5. Give *occupations* as fully as you can, stating not only the occupation but the kind of industry in which employed (as for the Census). Give the normal occupation whether at the moment employed in it or not; if there has been more than one such occupation, give them in order and number them.

6. Under the *first job* give the first job on starting life, not vacation or week-end work or other occasional jobs while at school.

7. Under *place of education* enter the kind of school ("Elementary," "Secondary," "Private," etc.) or "University."

8. Put down nothing of which you are not sure. If you are in doubt about a fact or a date, try to make sure by asking some member of your family who knows it. If you cannot make sure, write "Not known."

9. If you spoil a form or want to keep a duplicate, or want more forms for friends, you can get additional forms by sending a postcard to the B.B.C. Persuade as many of your friends as you can to fill in Family Forms.

10. If there is anything in the form which is not clear, write for an explanation to SIR WILLIAM BEVERIDGE, c/o B.B.C., Portland Place, London, W.1.

11. See next page for instructions on "Returning the Form."

APPENDIX

RETURNING THE FORM

When this form, or so much of it as any family is able to answer, has been filled in, it should be posted to Sir William Beveridge, c/o B.B.C., Portland Place, London, W.1. Stamped addressed envelopes for return will be sent out with most of the forms, but an ordinary envelope can be used. The sender's initials or name (real or assumed), with full postal address, should be written, for reference if necessary, on the back of the envelope in which the form is returned. As soon as the envelope is received at the B.B.C., the envelope and the form will both be numbered and will then be separated, the form being sent on to the London School of Economics, where it will be worked on and the results tabulated. If there is any point in the answers which wants clearing up, it will be possible by referring to the number on the form to have a communication sent to you, but no one who examines the form will have any idea of what particular family it refers to. The initials and address outside the envelope are not essential, since the answers, if they are all correct and clear, will have value. There is, however, the risk that, owing to some small point which is not clear in the answers and which it will then be impossible to clear up, the answers cannot be used.

A
REFERENCE

Town where family lives, or County, if not in a Town.

Occupation of Husband. (*See* Note 5.)

Whether Wage-Earner, Salaried, Employer, or on Own Account.

Income Classification. Write 1, 2, 3, 4, or 5, according as the total yearly family income is:

1. £150 or less
2. above £150 up to £300
3. above £300 up to £500
4. above £500 up to £800
5. above £800.

Include in your reckoning all income, whether earned or from interest, etc., of all members of family living at home, and the yearly value of the house occupied if it is owned by you.

B
HUSBAND AND WIFE

Year and month of marriage and of births of husband and wife.

Country of birth of husband and wife.

Full-Time Education (*see* Note 7): 1. Age of completing. 2. Place of completing. 3. Did it involve living away from home?

Details of Scholarships or Free Places won. If won but not taken up, say so.

Age of leaving parents' home.

Is this the first marriage of *both* husband and wife? If either was married before, fill up section C.

State whether or not husband and wife were cousins or otherwise related.

If either partner is dead, say which and give month and year of death.

If partners have separated, say how and give month and year of separation.

C

FORMER MARRIAGES OF EITHER PARTNER

The questions can be answered for either the husband or the wife, or for both.

Month and year of marriage and of ending of marriage.

Cause of ending (death or otherwise).

Number of children born.

Former Partner: age at marriage, whether related or not.

D

ALL CHILDREN OF MARRIAGE IN SECTION B

In order of birth, living and dead. If no children have been born, say "None."

State sex, first name or initials, day, month, and year of birth.

If *living with parents*, state "at home." If *left home*, state year of leaving and reason. If *dead*, state "dead" and exact date of death.

Full-Time Education: 1. Present place, or last place, if complete. (*See* Note 7.) 2. Does or did it involve living away from home? 3. If complete, state year of completing.

Details of Scholarships or Free Places won. If won but not taken up, say so.

If child has married, give month and year of marriage.

E

OCCUPATIONS AND EARNINGS

HUSBAND

Occupation. (*See* Note 5.)

Whether Wage-Earner, Salaried, Employer, or on Own Account.

Earnings in a normal week.

Reasons for choosing this occupation.

His First Job. (*See* Note 6.)

Age at which got. How long kept. Nature of job.

How got? (Whether through father, through mother, through other relations, through friends, through school, through Labour Exchange, by advertisement, by seeing notice in street, in some other way.)

WIFE

1. *Before Marriage:*

Paid Occupation (if none, say "None"). (*See* Note 5.)

Whether full-time or part-time job.

The remaining questions are the same as for the husband.

2. *After Marriage.* (*If none, say "None"; if same as before, say "Same"; if different, give details below.*)

State Paid Occupation and about how many hours a week this work keeps wife from home.

Whether Wage-Earner, Salaried, Employer, or on Own Account.

Whether full-time or part-time job.

What arrangements are made for house-work and care of the children.

Earnings in a normal week.

If occupied in paid work since marriage, state reasons for working in order of importance (whether to meet immediate needs, to be independent, to provide for old age, to provide for education of children, to get pocket money, to have something to do, because of interest in the work, for any other reason).

If the paid occupation named above has been given up at some time after marriage, state time and reason.

OCCUPIED CHILDREN

State first name or initials and whether living at home.

Occupation and whether Wage-Earner, Salaried, Employer, or on Own Account.

Earnings in a normal week.

Weekly contribution to family expenditure.

Reason for choosing occupation.

First job. (*The note and questions are as under "Husband."*)

F

FAMILY EXPENDITURE

How do husband and wife arrange money matters, e.g.—
  Common Purse, or fixed allowance from him (what does it cover?).

  If wife is not earning, has she any income other than what her husband allows her. If you have no objection, state amount.

If any relations sharing the home contribute to its expenses, give particulars.

If any allowance is being made to any child or relation away from home, give particulars.

How much paid domestic help is there in the home, and how does this compare with home of wife's parents.

G

HUSBAND'S AND WIFE'S PARENTS

The questions to be answered twice, once for the husband and once for the wife.

Month and year of marriage and of birth of both father and mother, and of death if either has died.

Country of birth of father and mother.

If both parents are living, say whether they are living together or separate.

If either or both are living, say whether living in own home, with a son, with a daughter, or elsewhere.

Father's Occupation.

Whether Wage-Earner, Salaried, Employer, or on Own Account.

If mother had any paid occupation, state nature and period (giving date of commencement and termination) *a*. before marriage; *b*. after marriage.

Father's Father's Occupation.

Whether Wage-Earner, Salaried, Employer, or on Own Account.

Mother's Father's Occupation.

Whether Wage-Earner, Salaried, Employer, or on Own Account.

H

LIST OF HUSBAND'S AND WIFE'S BROTHERS AND SISTERS

Include living and dead.

State sex. If full brother or sister, say so. If half-brother or sister, state common parent.

Month and year of birth.

Paid Occupation. (*Questions as above.*)

Full-Time Education: 1. Present place, or last place, if complete. (*See* Note 7.) 2. Does or did it involve living away from home? 3. If complete, state year of completing.

Details of Scholarships or Free Places won. If won but not taken up, say so.

If married, give year of marriage and number of children born. State whether living or dead. If dead, give date of death.

J

MEETING OF PARTNERS

State if husband and wife met at the home of husband's parents; at the home of wife's parents; at the house of friends; in a place of entertainment; at a school or university; on a holiday; in religious, political, or philanthropic activities; in some other way (name it).

If similar information can be given for the parents of the husband and wife or for their married children, this should be done.

K

REMARKS

L

FURTHER INFORMATION

Scientific investigations extending beyond the scope of this return are being conducted independently of the b.b.c. by the London School of Economics, through its Departments of Sociology and Social Biology, into various matters affecting the Family. If, with a view to helping the School in these investigations, you are able and willing to give further information on any of the subjects named below, please put a cross opposite such subjects, so that a further communication may be sent to you by the School under the same conditions of anonymity as apply to this return.

1. Family records of births, deaths, and marriages in earlier generations.
2. Family budgets now or in earlier times.
3. Twins (particularly any twins reared apart).
4. Factors affecting the size of the family.

If you put a cross here, it is essential to put your initials (or name) and full address outside the envelope when you return the Form. (See instructions for returning the Form.)

M

CHANGES AND FORCES IN FAMILY LIFE

Answer from your own experience, or that of your friends, not from what you have read in books or newspapers.

What are the chief changes, as between your parents' generation, your own generation, and the generation after yours in (*a*) The relations of husband and wife, including such matters as economic dependence of wife, choice of home or friends. (*b*) The relations of parents and children, including such matters as choice of careers, choice of partners, and claims to respect or obedience? (*c*) Family life generally, including such matters as relations of brothers and sisters, pooling of family income, house-work and uses of leisure?

What are the chief difficulties arising in family life, and what are the forces tending either (*a*) to bind the family more closely, (*b*) to loosen the ties between its members?

INDEX

Aberdeen, 75
Ability, inheritance of mental, 62
Adamson, Mrs. J. L., 7, 103–120, 134
Adoption of children, 56
  in America, 55
Africa—
  native races of, 73
  women's work in, 68
Age—
  of leaving home, 41
  retiring compulsory, 82
Albinism, 53, 57
Allowances, family, 110, 111
  and effect on the birth-rate, 113
America, 48, 55, 89, 96, 100
Aristotle, 32, 33, 102
Associations, voluntary, 101
Australia, tribal marriage customs in, 88

Bachelors, taxation of, 80
Barton, Mrs. Eleanor, 7, 67–82, 112
Baths, pithead, 70
Betrothal, child, 88
Biology, social, 53
Birth, order of, 60, 64
Birth-rate, 42, 115, 116
  coal-mining districts, 75
  cotton districts, 75
  fall in, 42, 44, 46, 48, 67, 72, 114, 128
  causes of, 49
  effects of, 49
Blackburn, 74, 75
Boswell, 86

Bradford, 74, 75
Breeding, selective, 52, 53, 54
British Broadcasting Corporation, 8, 9, 10, 13, 119, 137
Broadcast Adult Education, Central Council for, 10
Browne, F. W. Stella, 21

Cabinet, British, ages of, 47
California, 65
Careers, family influence on, 92, 94
Celibacy, effect on qualities in the stock, 54
Census, official, 40
Characters, recessive, 57
Cheshire, 38
Child, seventh, 41, 63
Childbirth, casualties in, 113
Children—
  allowances for, 79
  care of, improved conditions due to state, 77, 78
  desire for, 115
  economic assets, 79
  education of, 107
  elementary school, and Universities, 95
  employment of, 79
  essence of family, 40
  influence of parents on, 91
  psychology of, 91, 92
Chinese, method of reckoning age, 51
Civil service, origin of recruits to, 95
Classes, movements between, 94

INDEX

Cloth-makers, Yorkshire, 68
Cochrane's case, 28 *n.*
Colour blindness, 53
Cousin marriages, 56, 57, 60

Dalton, Dr. Hugh, 7, 67–82, 112
Darwin, Major Leonard, 99
Death-rate, fall in, 48
Deficiency, mental, 62
Defoe, 68
Demand, economic, dependence on growth of population, 47
Dependence, economic, of wives, 118
Descent, matrilineal, 24
Devices, labour-saving, 112
Dialogues, nature of, 8
Dilly, Mr., 105
Districts, dominated by industry, 74, 75
Dumbarton, 126
Durham, 74, 75

Economic Journal, 94
Economic conditions, change in, 30
Economica, 38 *n.*
Economics, London School of, 9, 10, 38, 50, 79, 80, 81, 96
Edinburgh, 126
Education, State, 90
Emancipation, economic, and political, 108
England, 38, 67, 125, 126, 139
Essex, 125
Eugenics, 99
Eugenics Society, President of, 99
Exchanges, Labour, 90

Factories, women in, 68
Family allowances, 79, 110, 111
  attitude of Trade Unions to, 80
  experiments at London School of Economics, 80, 81
  in New Zealand, 80, 81
Family—
  and inherited ability, 98
  attacks on, 102, 116
  changes and forces in life of, 122, 130, 131
  importance to individual, 19, 20
  investigation by B.B.C., 65
  large, revolt against, 112
  Law, change in, 28
  less clannishness in, 135
  management of income of, 65, 107
  order in, 41, 64
  size of, reasons for, 50
  stages of development, 21, 22
  State interest in, 23, 101
  State provision for, 79
Fertility, 64
Fife, 126
Forms, Family—
  compared with census, 40
  distribution of returns, 123, 126
  income of families, 127
  marriages of cousins, 57
  marriages on Forms returned, 123
  number returned, 123
  numbers used, 11, 13, 136, 137, 138
  Press criticism, 10–12, 83
  procedure for issue, 10, 13
  purpose, 31, 32
  request for, 137
  Section J, 83, 84, 90
  wage-earners, under-represented on returns, 127

Galton, Francis, 98, 99, 100
Ginsberg, Professor M., 7, 83–102
Guardianship, mothers' right to, 26

Haldane, Professor, 47
Heredity, 53
Hobhouse, Professor, 87
Hogben, Professor L. T., 59 n.
Home, leisure in, 112

Ibos, 89
Income—
  equality of, 99
  family, 107
  real, curve in, 46
Industry, growth of, 39
Instinct—
  maternal, 114, 115
  paternal, 114, 115
  sex, 114

Jackson, *Reg*. v., 27 n.
Johnson, Dr., views on marriage, 86, 87, 89

Ladder—
  the educational, 95
  the social, 93
Lanark, 126
Lancashire, 38, 69, 75, 77, 125, 126
Licences, wireless, percentage to population, 124 (chart), 125
Life, family—
  problems of, 67
  women in, 67
Life, social of savages, 23
Lincoln's Inn, 95
Linlithgow, 126
Listener, 47, 84

London, 38, 74, 75, 125
Lords, House of, 70

McCardie, Mr. Justice, 29 n., 104, 105, 108
Malinowski, Prof. B., 23, 24, 25
Marriage—
  a family affair, 89
  a free contract, 109
  African tribal customs, 89
  age at, 32, 33, 34, 36
  amongst primitive tribes, 85
  a personal affair, 85
  arranged by the family, 87
  choice of partners, 83, 135
  consent of women, 87
  cross-cousin custom of, 86
  customs, 85
  effect of—
    economic conditions on, 37
    occupation on age of, 36
    employment of women, effect of, on age, 37
  family influence on, 83, 85
  importance of, 83
  of minors, 89
  partners' meeting, 83, 129
  Royal, 85
  sayings about, 105
  seasons of, 37
Marriage-rate, fluctuation in, 44
Middlesbrough, 75
Middlesex, 125
Midlands, 70, 125, 126
Mill, John Stuart, 93
Mobility, occupational, 92, 94
Mongolism, 62 n.
Mothers and State social services, 78
Motive, family as an economic, 117
Müller-Lyer, Dr., 21

INDEX

Nature, 41, 51–65, 98
Newsholme, Sir Arthur, 42
Nurture, 41, 51–65, 98

Observer, 115
Occupations—
  change in, 129
  choice of, 130
  family influence on choice, 90
  necessity as factor in choice, 130
  of husbands, 126, 127
  parents' choice of, 130
  parents' influence on ,130
  persistence in, 129
  reasons for choosing, 90
Opportunity, equality of, 99, 100
Over-population, 46
Over-production, 48

Parents—
  ages of, at birth of children, 60
  occupation of, 93
  prospect of children, effect of age on, 41
  relation between age and size of family, 42
Patrilocal, 24
Pensions, 82
  old age, 81
Place v. *Searle*, 29
Plato, 102, 110
Polygamy, 23
Population—
  age constitution of, 47
  disappearing, 113
  growth of, 39, 43
  maintenance of, 114
  pressure of on subsistence, 43
  problems, 39
  stationary, 47
Press, attitude to Enquiry, 11, 12

Pressure, economic, 108
Property Act, Married Women's, 27, 30

Recessive characters, 53, 57
Registrar-General, 33, 34, 36 *n*.
Renfrew, 126
Revolution, Industrial, 39, 69
Rockefeller Foundation, 65
Rome, power of father, 20, 22
Russia, 110

Sankey, Lord, 86
Saunders, Professor Carr, 115, 116
Scholarship children, 62
Scholarships, 40, 41
  State, 100
  system, 95
  changes in, 62
  training for, 62
School-leaving age, 78, 79
Scotland, 67, 125, 126
Seligman, Professor, 84
Service, domestic, 130
Sexes, equality of, 103, 104, 107, 109, 110, 116, 118
Shaw, Bernard, 102
Social science, 12
  experiments in, 56
State, loyalty to, 110
State, relation to families, 100, 101
Stirling, 126
Stoke, 74
Students, 96
  University, receiving State assistance, 96
Succession, law of, 26
Sunderland, 75

Tadpoles, nurture in, 55
Tammany, 101

Teachers, university, 82
Telescope, compared to experiment in social science, 65
Thackeray, 61
Theory, the Russian, 109, 110, 116, 117, 118
Thomas, Miss Dorothy S., 38
Trobriand Islanders, 23, 24, 25, 26
Twins—
 accidental, 58
 age of parents at birth of, 61
 characteristics of, 58, 59, 60
 identical, 58
 proportion of, to marriages, 59
 tendency to give birth to, 61
 the Castlewood, 61
 the Newcome, 61

Universities—
 and employers, 96
 expansion of, 96
 Report of the University Grants Committee, 96, 96 n.
 scholarships to the, 96

Wales, 33, 67, 125
Welfare, infant, 116
Wiltshire, 74, 75
Wireless—
 and middle classes, 139
 and working classes, 139
Wives, economic independence of, 117
Work—
 household, 112
 women's, 70, 71

Workshop—
 break-up of the home as, 69
 home as, 68
Women—
 and politics, 106
 and public life, 106
 economic dependence of, 118
 economic freedom of, 108, 110, 111
 emancipation of, 104, 109
 home building by, 112
 married—
  and public careers, 112
  and single, differentiation between, 71
  conditions in Lancashire, 77
  duties of, 73
  economic dependence of, 110, 111, 134
  effect on male employment, 74
  employment of, 49
  in labour market, competition of, 73
  legal position of, 26, 29
  opportunities for work, 75
  percentage working, 74
  prejudice against working of, 70, 71
  reasons for working, 71, 72
  relation between work and number of children, 77
  work and birth-rate, 75
  work outside the home, 67, 68, 70

Yorkshire, 125, 126

CPSIA information can be obtained
at www.ICGtesting.com
Printed in the USA
BVHW041951060319
541975BV00019B/78/P